WORKBOOK

PREPARED BY MOOSAA RICHARDSON

ثلاثة الأصول وأدلّتها

THE THREE FUNDAMENTAL PRINCIPLES & THEIR EVIDENCES

شيخ الإسلام محمد بن عبد الوهاب رحمه الله

BY SHAYKH AL-ISLAM MUHAMMAD IBN 'ABDIL-WAHHAAB

MASJID AS-SUNNAH
AN·NABAWIYYAH
THE GERMANTOWN MASJID

🌐 germantownmasjid.com   🐦 @Gtownmasjid

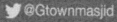
MW00452997

Copyright © 1440 (2019) by Moosaa Richardson.

All rights reserved. No part of this publication may be reproduced, distributed, or transmitted in any form or by any means, including photocopying, recording, or other electronic or mechanical methods, without the prior written permission of the copyright holder, except in the case of brief quotations embodied in critical reviews and certain other noncommercial uses permitted by copyright law.

Limited license to print in June 2019 granted to Germantown Masjid (Masjid as-Sunnah an-Nabawiyyah) in Germantown, Philadelphia (USA).

First Print Edition: Shawwaal 1440 (June 2019)

Second Print Edition: Thul-Qa'dah 1440 (July 2019)

The Three Fundamental Principles & Their Evidences, Workbook for Germantown Masjid's Summer Seminar (2019) / Author: Shaykh al-Islam Muhammad ibn 'Abdil-Wahhaab / Translator: Moosaa Richardson / Proofreader: Anwar Wright / Cover design: Awal Studio.

ISBN 978-1073082179

1. Nonfiction —Religion —Islam —Theology.

2. Education & Reference —Foreign Language Study —Arabic.

TABLE OF CONTENTS

INTRODUCTION

All praise is due to Allah, the Lord, Creator, and Sustainer of all things. May He raise the rank of and grant peace to His Prophet and final Messenger, Muhammad, and all of his respected family and noble companions.

If our priorities are in order, we should be using our few days in this worldly life to prepare for the inescapable reality coming at each and every one of us, according to Allah's Decree:

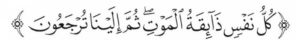

"Every soul shall taste death, and then unto Us you shall return." [29:57]

According to an authentic hadeeth collected by Imam Ahmad and others, from the report of al-Baraa' ibn 'Aazib (may Allah be pleased with him), the Messenger of Allah (may Allah raise his rank and grant him peace) mentioned that we will be questioned in our graves by two Angels; we will be asked about our Lord, our Religion, and our Prophet (may Allah raise his rank and grant him peace).

We ask Allah that He make us true believers who are blessed with stability in answering those questions, those whom He described in His Majestic Book:

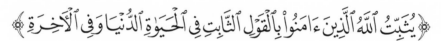

"Allah makes firm those who believe, by way of the firm statement, in this worldly life and in the Hereafter." [14:27]

As we beg and beseech our Lord for guidance and stability, we are required to take steps to prepare for that crucial event. The book, *Thalaathatul-Usool wa Adillatuhaa* (*The Three Fundamental Principles and Their Evidences*), is from the best and most focused writings on this topic, authored by one of the most knowledgeable and authoritative scholars of the past few centuries, Shaykh al-Islam Muhammad ibn 'Abdil-Wahhaab at-Tameemee (may Allah have Mercy on him).

Our brother, Ustaadh Hasan Somali (may Allah preserve him), and the community of Masjid as-Sunnah an-Nabawiyyah in Germantown, Philadelphia, have done well in selecting this book for this year's summer seminar. I am truly honored that he and his community entrusted me with preparing this workbook for the classes, and I ask Allah to grant us success, and to bless all of the scholars, students of knowledge, organizers, attendees, and supporters involved, and to make our cooperation a source of joy for us the Day we meet Him. I also ask Allah to reward my brother, Ustaadh Anwar Wright (may Allah preserve him), for his helpful proofreading of the workbook.

In this workbook, you will find the original Arabic text of the book, *The Three Fundamental Principles and Their Evidences*, paired with an English translation, spread out over 92 points, with ample space to take notes for each point. Appendices in the back provide a chain of transmission for the text, the complete text of the English translation, as well as three versions of the Arabic text:

- A fully voweled version (for beginners in Arabic)
- An unvoweled version (for intermediate Arabic students)
- A hand-written manuscript (for advanced Arabic students)

This summer's lessons are lined up to be a very unique opportunity for the English-speaking Muslims of the West (*in shaa' Allah*), as the speakers are students of knowledge who have studied the text under the people of knowledge. For example, Ustaadh Abul-Hasan Maalik (may Allah preserve him), during the era of Shaykh Muqbil (may Allah have Mercy on him) read the book to several of the teachers there, as did Ustaadh Rashee Barbee and Ustaadh Hasan Somali (may Allah preserve them both). Ustaadh Hasan also read the text and its explanation to Shaykh 'Ubayd al-Jaabiree (may Allah preserve him), who authorized him to translate it and teach it. His translation has been published by Salafi Publications. Our teachers have studied the text in formal and informal classes under the scholars and at universities and institutes of learning in various places. Of course, it goes without saying that our teachers have also read and listened to numerous explanations of the scholars for this important text. We pray that Allah blesses us with a great amount of benefit!

Beyond this summer's lessons, students are further encouraged to review this text further by committing to a more dedicated study, using one or more of the following recorded lessons in the English language, as found on www.SalafiSounds.com:

- 6 lessons taught by Shaykh Khaalid Thafeeree (may Allah preserve him), translated
- 50 lessons taught by Ustaadh Abu Talhah Daawood Burbank (may Allah have Mercy on him)
- 26 lessons taught by Ustaadh Abu Idrees (may Allah preserve him)

Additionally, there are 10 classes available on the Spreaker channel of Masjid Ahlul Quran wal-Hadeeth, taught by Ustaadh Kashif Khan (may Allah preserve him). Also, there are 63 recordings by Ustaadh Hamzah Abdur-Razzaaq on the Spreaker channel, "Masjidar-Razzaaq", in explanation of this text. There are also some classes on the Spreaker channel of al-Masjid al-Awwal in Pittsburgh ("Radio1MM").

I ask Allah that He grant me and you success in attaining His Pleasure and in drawing near to Him. May He -the Exalted and Most High- raise the rank of Muhammad and grant him and his family and companions an abundance of peace.

ABUL-'ABBAAS

MOOSAA RICHARDSON
Education Director
First Muslim Mosque
Pittsburgh, Pennsylvania
Email: MR@bakkah.net
Twitter: @1MMeducation

بسم الله الرحمن الرحيم وبه نستعين

اعلم رحمك الله انه يجب علينا تعلم اربع مسائل الأولى العلم وهو معرفة الله ومعرفة نبيه ومعرفة دين الاسلام بالادلة الثانية العمل به الثالثة الدعوة اليه الرابعة الصبر على الاذى فيه والدليل قوله تعالى بسم الله الرحمن الرحيم والعصر ان الانسان لفي خسر الا الذين آمنوا وعملوا الصالحات وتواصوا بالحق وتواصوا بالصبر قال الشافعي رحمه الله تعالى لو ما انزل الله حجة على خلقه الا هذه السورة لكفتهم قال البخاري رحمه الله تعالى باب العلم قبل القول والعمل والدليل قوله تعالى فاعلم انه لا اله الا الله فبدا بالعلم قبل القول والعمل اعلم رحمك الله ان الله وجب على كل مسلم ومسلمة تعلم ثلاث هذه المسائل والعمل بهن احداهن ان الله خلقنا ورزقنا ولم يتركنا هملا وارسل الينا رسولا فمن اطاعه دخل الجنة ومن عصاه دخل النار والدليل قوله تعالى انا ارسلنا اليكم رسولا شاهدا عليكم كما ارسلنا الى فرعون رسولا الثانية ان الله لا يرضى ان يشرك معه في عبادته احد لا نبي مرسل ولا ملك مقرب والدليل قوله تعالى وان المساجد لله فلا تدعوا مع الله احدا الثالثة ان من اطاع الرسول ووحد الله لا يجوز له موالاة من حاد الله ورسوله ولو كان اقرب قريب والدليل قوله تعالى لا تجد قوما يؤمنون بالله واليوم الآخر يوادون

For the complete manuscript, go to page 137.

POINT 1

An Introduction to the Text and its Author

POINT 2

FOUR ESSENTIAL MATTERS WE MUST LEARN

بِسْمِ اللهِ الرَّحْمَنِ الرَّحِيمِ، اعْلَمْ رَحِمَكَ اللهُ أَنَّهُ يَجِبُ عَلَيْنَا تَعَلُّمُ أَرْبَعِ مَسَائِلَ: الأُولَى العِلْمُ، وَهُوَ مَعْرِفَةُ اللهِ، وَمَعْرِفَةُ نَبِيِّهِ، وَمَعْرِفَةُ دِينِ الإِسْلَامِ بِالأَدِلَّةِ. الثَّانِيَةُ العَمَلُ بِهِ. الثَّالِثَةُ الدَّعْوَةُ إِلَيْهِ. الرَّابِعَةُ الصَّبْرُ عَلَى الأَذَى فِيهِ.

In the Name of Allah, the Most Merciful, the Ever Merciful: Know –may Allah have Mercy on you- that it is incumbent upon us to learn four matters: The first one is knowledge, which is awareness of Allah, awareness of His Prophet, and awareness of the Religion of Islam, with proofs. The second one is acting by it. The third one is calling to it. The fourth one is being patient with the harms that come with that.

POINT 3

One Short Soorah as Comprehensive Proof

وَالدَّلِيلُ قَوْلُهُ تَعَالَى: بِسْمِ اللهِ الرَّحْمَنِ الرَّحِيمِ، ﴿وَالْعَصْرِ ۝ إِنَّ الْإِنسَانَ لَفِى خُسْرٍ ۝ إِلَّا الَّذِينَ ءَامَنُوا وَعَمِلُوا الصَّالِحَاتِ وَتَوَاصَوْا بِالْحَقِّ وَتَوَاصَوْا بِالصَّبْرِ ۝﴾. قَالَ الشَّافِعِيُّ رَحِمَهُ اللهُ تَعَالَى: لَوْ مَا أَنْزَلَ اللهُ حُجَّةً عَلَى خَلْقِهِ إِلَّا هَذِهِ السُّورَةَ لَكَفَتْهُمْ.

The proof is His Statement, Exalted is He: "In the Name of Allah, the Most Merciful, the Ever Merciful. By the passing of time, Mankind is indeed in a state of loss, except for those who believe, perform righteous deeds, admonish one another with the Truth, and admonish one another with patience." [103:1-3] Ash-Shaafi'ee –may Allah, the Exalted, have Mercy on him- said: Had Allah not sent down any proof upon His Creation other than this Soorah, it would have sufficed them.

POINT 4

KNOWLEDGE PRECEDES STATEMENTS AND ACTIONS

وَقَالَ البُخَارِيُّ رَحِمَهُ اللهُ تَعَالَى: بَابُ العِلْمِ قَبْلَ القَوْلِ وَالعَمَلِ، وَالدَّلِيلُ قَوْلُهُ تَعَالَى:

﴿فَٱعْلَمْ أَنَّهُ لَا إِلَهَ إِلَّا ٱللَّهُ وَٱسْتَغْفِرْ لِذَنْبِكَ﴾، فَبَدَأَ بِالعِلْمِ قَبْلَ القَوْلِ وَالعَمَلِ.

And al-Bukhaaree –may Allah, the Exalted, have Mercy on him- said: Chapter: Knowledge Precedes Statements and Actions; the Proof is His Statement, Exalted is He: "So have knowledge (O Muhammad) that there is no one worthy of worship other than Allah, and seek forgiveness for your sin." [47:19] He began with knowledge, before (mentioning) statements or actions.

POINT 5

THE PURPOSE OF MANKIND'S CREATION

اعْلَمْ رَحِمَكَ اللهُ أَنَّهُ يَجِبُ عَلَى كُلِّ مُسْلِمٍ وَمُسْلِمَةٍ تَعَلُّمُ ثَلَاثِ هَذِهِ الْمَسَائِلِ وَالْعَمَلُ بِهِنَّ: الْأُوْلَى: أَنَّ اللهَ خَلَقَنَا وَرَزَقَنَا وَلَمْ يَتْرُكْنَا هَمَلًا، بَلْ أَرْسَلَ إِلَيْنَا رَسُولًا، فَمَنْ أَطَاعَهُ دَخَلَ الْجَنَّةَ، وَمَنْ عَصَاهُ دَخَلَ النَّارَ.

Know –may Allah have Mercy on you- that it is incumbent upon every Muslim, male or female, to learn three of these matters and act upon them: Firstly, that Allah has created us, provided for us, and not left us without purpose. Instead, He has sent a Messenger to us; whoever obeys him goes to Paradise, and whoever disobeys him goes to the Fire.

POINT 6

MESSENGERS MUST BE OBEYED: THE PROOF

وَالدَّلِيلُ قَوْلُهُ تَعَالَى : ﴿ إِنَّا أَرْسَلْنَا إِلَيْكُمْ رَسُولًا شَاهِدًا عَلَيْكُمْ كَمَا أَرْسَلْنَا إِلَى فِرْعَوْنَ رَسُولًا ۝

فَعَصَى فِرْعَوْنُ الرَّسُولَ فَأَخَذْنَاهُ أَخْذًا وَبِيلًا ۝ ﴾ .

The proof is His Statement, Exalted is He: "Verily We have sent to you a Messenger as a witness over you, just as We sent to Pharaoh a Messenger. Yet, Pharaoh disobeyed the Messenger, so We seized him with a severe punishment." [73:16]

POINT 7

ALLAH IS NOT PLEASED WITH SHIRK

الثَّانِيَةُ: أَنَّ اللهَ لَا يَرْضَى أَنْ يُشْرَكَ مَعَهُ فِي عِبَادَتِهِ أَحَدٌ، لَا مَلَكٌ مُقَرَّبٌ،

وَلَا نَبِيٌّ مُرْسَلٌ.

The second one is that Allah is not pleased with any partners being associated with Him in worship, not even an Angel brought near, nor any Prophet sent forth as a Messenger.

15

POINT 8

THE ABSOLUTE PROHIBITION OF SHIRK

وَالدَّلِيلُ قَوْلُهُ تَعَالَى: ﴿وَأَنَّ ٱلْمَسَٰجِدَ لِلَّهِ فَلَا تَدْعُوا۟ مَعَ ٱللَّهِ أَحَدًا﴾.

The proof is His Statement, Exalted is He: "And verily the masaajid are for Allah [alone], so do not call upon anyone along with Allah." [72:18]

POINT 9

RELIGIOUS LOYALTY MUST BE FOR ALLAH'S SAKE ALONE

الثَّالِثَةُ: أَنَّ مَنْ أَطَاعَ الرَّسُولَ وَوَحَّدَ اللهَ لَا يَجُوزُ لَهُ مُوَالَاةُ مَنْ حَادَّ اللهَ وَرَسُولَهُ،
وَلَوْ كَانَ أَقْرَبَ قَرِيبٍ.

The third one is that whoever obeys the Messenger and singles out Allah [in worship] is not allowed to have a religious loyalty to anyone who staunchly opposes Allah and His Messenger, even if he were the closest of kin.

POINT 10

TRUE BELIEVERS AND THEIR RELIGIOUS LOYALTY

وَالدَّلِيلُ قَوْلُهُ تَعَالَى: ﴿لَا تَجِدُ قَوْمًا يُؤْمِنُونَ بِاللَّهِ وَالْيَوْمِ الْآخِرِ يُوَادُّونَ مَنْ حَادَّ اللَّهَ وَرَسُولَهُ وَلَوْ كَانُوا آبَاءَهُمْ أَوْ أَبْنَاءَهُمْ أَوْ إِخْوَانَهُمْ أَوْ عَشِيرَتَهُمْ أُولَئِكَ كَتَبَ فِي قُلُوبِهِمُ الْإِيمَانَ وَأَيَّدَهُمْ بِرُوحٍ مِنْهُ وَيُدْخِلُهُمْ جَنَّاتٍ تَجْرِي مِنْ تَحْتِهَا الْأَنْهَارُ خَالِدِينَ فِيهَا رَضِيَ اللَّهُ عَنْهُمْ وَرَضُوا عَنْهُ أُولَئِكَ حِزْبُ اللَّهِ أَلَا إِنَّ حِزْبَ اللَّهِ هُمُ الْمُفْلِحُونَ﴾.

The proof is His Statement, Exalted is He: "You do not find any people who believe in Allah and the Last Day loving those who staunchly oppose Allah and His Messenger, even if they were their fathers, children, brothers, or close kin. For such people, He has written for faith to enter their hearts, and He has aided them with a Rooh (i.e. proofs and guidance) from Himself. He shall place them in gardens under which rivers flow, abiding therein forever. He is pleased with them, and they are pleased with Him. Such people are the Hizb (Party) of Allah. Nay, the Hizb of Allah are indeed the successful ones." [58:22]

POINT 11

THE RELIGION OF IBRAAHEEM: ISLAMIC MONOTHEISM

اعْلَمْ أَرْشَدَكَ اللهُ لِطَاعَتِهِ: أَنَّ الحَنِيفِيَّةَ مِلَّةَ إِبْرَاهِيمَ أَنْ تَعْبُدَ اللهَ وَحْدَهُ مُخْلِصًا لَهُ الدِّينَ.

Know –may Allah guide you to His obedience- that Haneefiyyah (pure Islamic monotheism), the Religion of Ibraaheem, is that you worship Allah alone, dedicating yourself in Religion to Him exclusively.

POINT 12

ALLAH CREATED MANKIND TO WORSHIP HIM

وَبِذَلِكَ أَمَرَ اللهُ جَمِيعَ النَّاسِ وَخَلَقَهُمْ لَهَا، قَالَ تَعَالَى: ﴿وَمَا خَلَقْتُ الْجِنَّ وَالْإِنسَ إِلَّا لِيَعْبُدُونِ﴾، وَمَعْنَى يَعْبُدُونَ: يُوَحِّدُونَ.

That is what Allah has ordered all of Mankind with and created them for. He, the Exalted, has said: "And I have not created the Jinn nor Mankind except for them to worship Me (alone)." [51:56] And the meaning of "to worship" is: to single out [Allah].

POINT 13

THE GREATEST OF ALL OBLIGATIONS

وَأَعْظَمُ مَا أَمَرَ اللهُ بِهِ: التَّوْحِيدُ، وَهُوَ إِفْرَادُ اللهِ بِالعِبَادَةِ.

*The greatest of all things that Allah has ordered is towheed,
which is to single out Allah with all acts of worship.*

POINT 14

THE MOST SEVERELY FORBIDDEN SIN

وَأَعْظَمُ مَا نَهَى عَنْهُ: الشِّرْكُ، وَهُوَ دَعْوَةُ غَيْرِهِ مَعَهُ.

And the greatest (i.e. most sinful) thing He has forbidden is shirk, which is to call upon other than Him.

POINT 15

A Specific Order and a Broad Prohibition

والدَّلِيلُ قَوْلُهُ تَعَالَى: ﴿وَاعْبُدُوا اللَّهَ وَلَا تُشْرِكُوا بِهِ شَيْئًا﴾.

The proof is His Statement, Exalted is He: "Worship Allah (alone),
and do not associate a single partner with Him." [4:36]

POINT 16

WHAT ARE THE THREE FUNDAMENTAL PRINCIPLES?

فَإِذَا قِيلَ لَكَ: مَا الْأُصُولُ الثَّلَاثَةُ الَّتِي يَجِبُ عَلَى الْإِنْسَانِ مَعْرِفَتُهَا؟

فَقُلْ: مَعْرِفَةُ العَبْدِ رَبَّهُ، وَدِينَهُ، وَنَبِيَّهُ مُحَمَّدًا صَلَّى اللهُ عَلَيْهِ وَسَلَّمَ.

If you are asked: "What are the three fundamental principles which all of Mankind must have awareness of?" Then say: The worshipper's awareness of his Lord, his Religion, and his Prophet, Muhammad –may Allah raise his rank and grant him peace-.

THE FIRST OF THE THREE FUNDAMENTAL PRINCIPLES

فَإِذَا قِيلَ لَكَ: مَنْ رَبُّكَ؟ فَقُلْ: رَبِّيَ اللهُ الَّذِي رَبَّانِي وَرَبَّى جَمِيعَ العَالَمِينَ بِنِعْمَتِهِ، وَهُوَ مَعْبُودِي، لَيْسَ لِي مَعْبُودٌ سِوَاهُ.

If you are asked: "Who is your Lord?" Then say: "My Lord is Allah, the One who has sustained me and the entire universe by His Blessings. He (Alone) is my object of worship; I have no object of worship other than Him."

POINT 18

THE ONE TRUE LORD, CREATOR, AND SUSTAINER

وَالدَّلِيلُ قَوْلُهُ تَعَالَى: ﴿ٱلْحَمْدُ لِلَّهِ رَبِّ ٱلْعَلَمِينَ﴾،

وَكُلُّ مَا سِوَى اللهِ عَالَمٌ، وَأَنَا وَاحِدٌ مِنْ ذَلِكَ العَالَمِ.

The proof is His Statement, Exalted is He: "All praise is due to Allah, the Lord, Creator, and Sustainer of the 'Aalameen." [1:1] And everything besides Allah is [called] an 'aalam (a created thing), and I am one of that 'aalam.

POINT 19

HOW A WORSHIPPER KNOWS ABOUT HIS LORD

فَإِذَا قِيلَ لَكَ: بِمَ عَرَفْتَ رَبَّكَ؟ فَقُلْ: بِآيَاتِهِ وَمَخْلُوقَاتِهِ.

وَمِنْ آيَاتِهِ: اللَّيْلُ، وَالنَّهَارُ، وَالشَّمْسُ، وَالقَمَرُ. وَمِنْ مَخْلُوقَاتِهِ:

السَّمَاوَاتُ السَّبْعُ، وَالأَرَضُونَ السَّبْعُ، وَمَنْ فِيهِنَّ، وَمَا بَيْنَهُمَا.

If you are asked: "How do you know about your Lord?" Then say: "By way of His great signs and creation. From His great signs are the night, the day, the Sun, and the Moon. And from His creation are the seven heavens, the seven earths, all those within them, and all that is between them."

POINT 20

AMONG THE GREATEST OF ALLAH'S SIGNS

وَالدَّلِيلُ قَوْلُهُ تَعَالَى : ﴿ وَمِنْ ءَايَتِهِ ٱلَّيْلُ وَٱلنَّهَارُ وَٱلشَّمْسُ وَٱلْقَمَرُ لَا تَسْجُدُوا۟ لِلشَّمْسِ وَلَا لِلْقَمَرِ وَٱسْجُدُوا۟ لِلَّهِ ٱلَّذِى خَلَقَهُنَّ إِن كُنتُمْ إِيَّاهُ تَعْبُدُونَ ﴾ .

The proof is His Statement, Exalted is He: "And from His Signs are the night, the day, the Sun, and the Moon. Do not prostrate to the Sun or the Moon, but instead prostrate to the One who created them, if it is Him that you truly worship." [41:37]

POINT 21

THE CREATION AND THE COMMAND BELONG TO ALLAH

وَقَوْلُهُ تَعَالَى: ﴿ إِنَّ رَبَّكُمُ ٱللَّهُ ٱلَّذِى خَلَقَ ٱلسَّمَٰوَٰتِ وَٱلْأَرْضَ فِى سِتَّةِ أَيَّامٖ ثُمَّ ٱسْتَوَىٰ عَلَى ٱلْعَرْشِ يُغْشِى ٱلَّيْلَ ٱلنَّهَارَ يَطْلُبُهُۥ حَثِيثٗا وَٱلشَّمْسَ وَٱلْقَمَرَ وَٱلنُّجُومَ مُسَخَّرَٰتِۭ بِأَمْرِهِۦٓ أَلَا لَهُ ٱلْخَلْقُ وَٱلْأَمْرُ تَبَارَكَ ٱللَّهُ رَبُّ ٱلْعَٰلَمِينَ ﴾ .

And His Statement, Exalted is He: "Verily, your Lord is Allah, the One who created the heavens and the earth in six days; He then ascended above the Throne. He brings the night as a covering over the day, coming after it rapidly. The Sun, the Moon, and the stars are all placed in [our] service, by His Command. Nay, to Him (Alone) belong the Creation and the Command. Blessed is He, the Lord of all the 'Aalameen." [7:54]

POINT 22

THE LORD AND CREATOR ALONE DESERVES WORSHIP

وَالرَّبُّ هُوَ الْمَعْبُودُ، وَالدَّلِيلُ قَوْلُهُ تَعَالَى : ﴿يَا أَيُّهَا النَّاسُ اعْبُدُوا رَبَّكُمُ الَّذِي خَلَقَكُمْ

وَالَّذِينَ مِنْ قَبْلِكُمْ لَعَلَّكُمْ تَتَّقُونَ ۞ الَّذِي جَعَلَ لَكُمُ الْأَرْضَ فِرَاشًا وَالسَّمَاءَ بِنَاءً وَأَنْزَلَ مِنَ السَّمَاءِ

مَاءً فَأَخْرَجَ بِهِ مِنَ الثَّمَرَاتِ رِزْقًا لَكُمْ فَلَا تَجْعَلُوا لِلَّهِ أَنْدَادًا وَأَنْتُمْ تَعْلَمُونَ ۞﴾ .

قَالَ ابْنُ كَثِيرٍ : الْخَالِقُ لِهَذِهِ الْأَشْيَاءِ هُوَ الْمُسْتَحِقُّ لِلْعِبَادَةِ .

The Lord is the only One worthy of worship; the proof is His Statement, Exalted is He: "O Mankind! Worship your Lord who has created you and all of those before you, so you might attain piety. [He is] The One who made the earth a place of comfort for you, and the sky as a canopy. And He sent down from the sky rainwater and brought forth harvests as provisions for you. So do not set up rivals unto Allah, whilst you have knowledge." [2:22] Ibn Katheer said, "The Creator of these things is the (only) One worthy of worship."

POINT 23

THE THREE LEVELS: ISLAM, EEMAAN, AND IHSAAN

وَأَنْوَاعُ العِبَادَةِ الَّتِي أَمَرَ اللهُ بِهَا مِثْلُ الإِسْلَامِ، وَالإِيْمَانِ، وَالإِحْسَانِ.

The various kinds of worship which Allah has ordered are like: Islam, Eemaan, and Ihsaan.

POINT 24

ALL ACTS OF WORSHIP ARE DUE TO ALLAH ALONE

وَمِنْهُ الدُّعَاءُ، وَالْخَوْفُ، وَالرَّجَاءُ، وَالتَّوَكُّلُ، وَالرَّغْبَةُ، وَالرَّهْبَةُ، وَالْخُشُوعُ،

وَالْخَشْيَةُ، وَالإِنَابَةُ، وَالاسْتِعَانَةُ، وَالاسْتِعَاذَةُ، وَالاسْتِغَاثَةُ، وَالذَّبْحُ، وَالنَّذْرُ،

وَغَيْرُ ذَلِكَ مِنَ العِبَادَةِ الَّتِي أَمَرَ اللهُ بِهَا، كُلُّهَا لِلَّهِ.

From them is: Supplication, fear, hope, trust, ambition, awe, humility, knowledge-based fear, repentance, seeking assistance, refuge, and relief, slaughtering (animals), vows, and other kinds of worship that Allah has ordered; all of that is for Allah (alone).

POINT 25

PLACES OF PROSTRATION ARE FOR ALLAH ALONE

وَالدَّلِيلُ قَوْلُهُ تَعَالَى: ﴿وَأَنَّ ٱلْمَسَٰجِدَ لِلَّهِ فَلَا تَدْعُوا۟ مَعَ ٱللَّهِ أَحَدًا﴾.

The proof is His Statement, Exalted is He: "And verily the masaajid are for Allah [alone], so do not call upon anyone along with Allah." [72:18]

POINT 26

DIRECTING WORSHIP TO OTHER THAN ALLAH

فَمَنْ صَرَفَ مِنْهَا شَيْئًا لِغَيْرِ اللهِ فَهُوَ مُشْرِكٌ كَافِرٌ.

Whoever directs any of that to other than Allah is a polytheist disbeliever.

POINT 27

CALLING UPON FALSE DEITIES IS DISBELIEF

وَالدَّلِيلُ قَوْلُهُ تَعَالَى : ﴿وَمَن يَدْعُ مَعَ ٱللَّهِ إِلَٰهًا ءَاخَرَ لَا بُرْهَٰنَ لَهُۥ بِهِۦ فَإِنَّمَا حِسَابُهُۥ عِندَ رَبِّهِۦٓ إِنَّهُۥ لَا يُفْلِحُ ٱلْكَٰفِرُونَ﴾.

The proof is His Statement, Exalted is He: "And whosoever calls upon another deity besides Allah, for which he has no proof, his account will be with his Lord alone. Verily, the disbelievers are not successful." [23:117]

POINT 28

SUPPLICATION IS THE CORE OF WORSHIP

وَفِي الحَدِيثِ: الدُّعَاءُ مُخُّ العِبَادَةِ.

And in the hadeeth: "Supplication is the core of worship."

POINT 29

ALLAH REFERS TO SUPPLICATION AS WORSHIP

وَالدَّلِيلُ قَوْلُهُ تَعَالَى: ﴿وَقَالَ رَبُّكُمُ ٱدْعُونِي أَسْتَجِبْ لَكُمْ إِنَّ ٱلَّذِينَ يَسْتَكْبِرُونَ عَنْ عِبَادَتِي سَيَدْخُلُونَ جَهَنَّمَ دَاخِرِينَ ﴾.

The proof is also His Statement, Exalted is He: "And your Lord has said: Call upon Me; I shall answer you. Verily, those who arrogantly refuse to worship Me shall enter the Hellfire, in humiliation." [40:60]

POINT 30

FEARING ALLAH ALONE IS A FORM OF WORSHIP

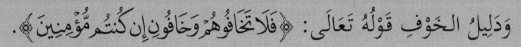

The proof for fear (as a form of worship) is His Statement, Exalted is He:
"So do not fear them, but instead fear Me, if you are indeed believers." [3:175]

POINT 31

THE WORSHIP OF HOPE AND ASPIRATION

وَدَلِيلُ الرَّجَاءِ قَوْلُهُ تَعَالَى : ﴿فَمَن كَانَ يَرْجُواْ لِقَآءَ رَبِّهِ فَلْيَعْمَلْ عَمَلًا صَلِحًا وَلَا يُشْرِكْ بِعِبَادَةِ رَبِّهِ أَحَدًا﴾ .

The proof for hope (as a form of worship) is His Statement, Exalted is He: "So whoever hopes for the meeting with his Lord, let him work righteous deeds and not associate any partner in the worship of his Lord." [18:110]

POINT 32

THE WORSHIP OF TRUST AND RELIANCE

وَدَلِيلُ التَّوَكُّلِ قَوْلُهُ تَعَالَى: ﴿وَعَلَى ٱللَّهِ فَتَوَكَّلُوٓاْ إِن كُنتُم مُّؤۡمِنِينَ﴾؛

﴿وَمَن يَتَوَكَّلۡ عَلَى ٱللَّهِ فَهُوَ حَسۡبُهُۥٓ﴾.

The proof for trust (as a form of worship) is His Statement, Exalted is He:
"So upon Allah (alone) place your trust, if you are indeed believers." [10:84]
"And whoever places his trust in Allah (alone), He will suffice him." [65:3]

POINT 33

HOPE AND FEARFUL AWE ARE FORMS OF WORSHIP

وَدَلِيلُ الرَّغْبَةِ وَالرَّهْبَةِ وَالْخُشُوعِ قَوْلُهُ تَعَالَى: ﴿إِنَّهُمْ كَانُوا يُسَارِعُونَ فِي الْخَيْرَاتِ وَيَدْعُونَنَا رَغَبًا وَرَهَبًا وَكَانُوا لَنَا خَاشِعِينَ﴾.

The proof for awe and humility (as forms of worship) is His Statement, Exalted is He:"Verily, they had hastened into good actions and called upon Us out of hope and fearful awe, surrendering unto Us in humility." [21:90]

POINT 34

KNOWLEDGE-BASED FEAR IS A FORM OF WORSHIP

وَدَلِيلُ الْخَشْيَةِ قَوْلُهُ تَعَالَى : ﴿فَلَا تَخْشَوْهُمْ وَاخْشَوْنِ﴾، الآيَةُ.

The proof for knowledge-based fear (as a form of worship) is His Statement,
Exalted is He: "So do not fear them, but instead fear Me..." [5:3]

POINT 35

REPENTANCE IS A FORM OF WORSHIP

وَدَلِيلُ الإِنَابَةِ قَوْلُهُ تَعَالَى: ﴿وَأَنِيبُوا إِلَى رَبِّكُمْ وَأَسْلِمُوا لَهُ مِن قَبْلِ أَن يَأْتِيَكُمُ الْعَذَابُ ثُمَّ لَا تُنصَرُونَ﴾، الآيَةُ.

The proof for repentance (as a form of worship) is His Statement, Exalted is He: "And repent to your Lord, and submit unto Him (alone), before the punishment comes to you, after which you would never be aided..." [39:54]

POINT 36

SEEKING HELP AS A FORM OF WORSHIP

وَدَلِيلُ الِاسْتِعَانَةِ قَوْلُهُ تَعَالَى: ﴿ إِيَّاكَ نَعْبُدُ وَإِيَّاكَ نَسْتَعِينُ ﴾.

The proof for seeking assistance (as a form of worship) is His Statement, Exalted is He: "You Alone we worship; from You Alone we seek help." [1:4]

POINT 37

SEEKING ALLAH'S HELP IN ALL AFFAIRS

وَفِي الحَدِيثِ: ﴿إِذَا اسْتَعَنْتَ فَاسْتَعِنْ بِاللهِ.﴾

And in the hadeeth: "Whenever you seek help, seek the help of Allah."

POINT 38

SEEKING REFUGE AS A FORM OF WORSHIP

وَدَلِيلُ الِاسْتِعَاذَةِ قَوْلُهُ تَعَالَى: ﴿قُلْ أَعُوذُ بِرَبِّ النَّاسِ﴾.

The proof for seeking refuge (as a form of worship) is His Statement, Exalted is He: "Say: I seek refuge with the Lord of Mankind." [114:1]

POINT 39

SEEKING RELIEF AS A FORM OF WORSHIP

وَدَلِيلُ الاِسْتِغَاثَةِ قَوْلُهُ تَعَالَى: ﴿إِذْ تَسْتَغِيثُونَ رَبَّكُمْ فَٱسْتَجَابَ لَكُمْ﴾، الآيَةُ.

The proof for seeking relief (as a form of worship) is His Statement, Exalted is He: "Remember when you were seeking relief from your Lord, and He responded to your request..." [8:9]

POINT 40

SLAUGHTERING SACRIFICIAL ANIMALS IS WORSHIP

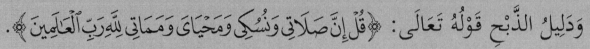

The proof for slaughtering (animals, as a form of worship) is His Statement, Exalted is He: "Say: Verily my prayer, my slaughtering (of sacrificial animals), my living, and my dying are all for Allah, the Lord of the 'Aalameen." [6:162]

POINT 41

SACRIFICING ANIMALS TO OTHER THAN ALLAH

وَمِنَ السُّنَّةِ: ﴿لَعَنَ اللهُ مَنْ ذَبَحَ لِغَيْرِ اللهِ.﴾

And from the Sunnah: "The curse of Allah is upon anyone who slaughters (a sacrificial animal) for other than Allah."

POINT 42

TAKING A VOW IS A FORM OF WORSHIP

وَدَلِيلُ النَّذْرِ قَوْلُهُ تَعَالَى : ﴿ يُوفُونَ بِالنَّذْرِ وَيَخَافُونَ يَوْمًا كَانَ شَرُّهُ مُسْتَطِيرًا ﴾ .

The proof for taking vows (as a form of worship) is His Statement, Exalted is He: "They fulfill their vows, and they fear a day, the evil of which is widespread." [76:7]

POINT 43

THE SECOND OF THE THREE FUNDAMENTAL PRINCIPLES

الأَصْلُ الثَّانِي: مَعْرِفَةُ دِيْنِ الإِسْلَامِ بِالأَدِلَّةِ، وَهُوَ الاِسْتِسْلَامُ لِلَّهِ بِالتَّوْحِيدِ، وَالاِنْقِيَادُ لَهُ بِالطَّاعَةِ، وَالخُلُوصُ مِنَ الشِّرْكِ.

The second fundamental principle is awareness of the Religion of Islam with proofs, which is submission to Allah with towheed, surrendering to Him with obedience, and absolving oneself entirely of shirk.

POINT 44

THE THREE LEVELS OF THE RELIGION

وَهُوَ ثَلَاثُ مَرَاتِبَ: الإِسْلَامُ، وَالإِيْمَانُ، وَالإِحْسَانُ، وَكُلُّ مَرْتَبَةٍ لَهَا أَرْكَانٌ.

And it (the Religion) is of three levels: Islam, Eemaan, and Ihsaan; each level has pillars.

POINT 45

THE FIVE PILLARS OF ISLAM

فَأَرْكَانُ الْإِسْلَامِ خَمْسَةٌ: شَهَادَةُ أَنْ لَا إِلَهَ إِلَّا اللهُ، وَأَنَّ مُحَمَّدًا رَسُولُ اللهِ، وَإِقَامُ الصَّلَاةِ، وَإِيتَاءُ الزَّكَاةِ، وَصَوْمُ رَمَضَانَ، وَحَجُّ بَيْتِ اللهِ الْحَرَامِ.

The pillars of Islam are five: [1] The testimony that no one deserves worship other than Allah and that Muhammad is His Messenger, [2] the establishment of prayer, [3] the payment of zakaat, [4] the fasting of Ramadhaan, and [5] making Hajj to the sacred House of Allah.

POINT 46

ALLAH HIMSELF TESTIFIES TO HIS ONENESS

فَدَلِيلُ الشَّهَادَةِ قَوْلُهُ تَعَالَى : ﴿شَهِدَ ٱللَّهُ أَنَّهُۥ لَآ إِلَٰهَ إِلَّا هُوَ وَٱلْمَلَٰٓئِكَةُ وَأُوْلُواْ ٱلْعِلْمِ قَآئِمًۢا بِٱلْقِسْطِ لَآ إِلَٰهَ إِلَّا هُوَ ٱلْعَزِيزُ ٱلْحَكِيمُ﴾.

The proof for the testimony is His Statement, Exalted is He: "Allah testifies that none have the right to be worshipped other than Him, and the Angels (also testify), and the people of knowledge, maintaining (His Creation) with Justice. No one has the right to be worshipped but Him, the All-Mighty, the Ever Wise." [3:18]

POINT 47

THE MEANING OF THE TESTIMONY OF TOHWEED

وَمَعْنَاهَا: لَا مَعْبُودَ بِحَقٍّ إِلَّا اللهُ وَحْدَهُ. وَلَا إِلَهَ: نَافِيًا جَمِيعَ مَا يُعْبَدُ

مِنْ دُونِ اللهِ؛ إِلَّا اللهُ: مُثْبِتًا العِبَادَةَ لِلَّهِ وَحْدَهُ لَا شَرِيكَ لَهُ فِي عِبَادَتِهِ،

كَمَا أَنَّهُ لَيْسَ لَهُ شَرِيكٌ فِي مُلْكِهِ.

And its meaning is: There is no deity deserving worship, other than Allah Alone. "Laa-elaaha" is a negation of all things worshipped beside Allah; "ill-Allah" is an affirmation of Allah's Right to be worshipped, which He shares with no one, just as none share in His Dominion.

POINT 48

A FINE EXAMPLE OF IMPLEMENATION OF TOWHEED

وَتَفْسِيرُهَا الَّذِي يُوَضِّحُهَا قَوْلُهُ تَعَالَى: ﴿وَإِذْ قَالَ إِبْرَاهِيمُ لِأَبِيهِ وَقَوْمِهِ إِنَّنِي بَرَاءٌ مِّمَّا تَعْبُدُونَ ﴿٢٦﴾ إِلَّا الَّذِي فَطَرَنِي فَإِنَّهُ سَيَهْدِينِ ﴿٢٧﴾ وَجَعَلَهَا كَلِمَةً بَاقِيَةً فِي عَقِبِهِ لَعَلَّهُمْ يَرْجِعُونَ ﴿٢٨﴾﴾ .

The explanation which clarifies that is His Statement, Exalted is He: "And [remember] when Ibraaheem said to his father and his people: 'I am free of all those you worship, except for the One who created me; He shall surely guide me.' And he made that a word remaining after him, in order for them to return (to it after straying)." [43:26]

POINT 49

وَقَوْلُهُ تَعَالَى : ﴿ قُلْ يَٰٓأَهْلَ ٱلْكِتَٰبِ تَعَالَوْاْ إِلَىٰ كَلِمَةٍ سَوَآءٍ بَيْنَنَا وَبَيْنَكُمْ أَلَّا نَعْبُدَ إِلَّا ٱللَّهَ وَلَا نُشْرِكَ بِهِۦ شَيْـًٔا وَلَا يَتَّخِذَ بَعْضُنَا بَعْضًا أَرْبَابًا مِّن دُونِ ٱللَّهِ فَإِن تَوَلَّوْاْ فَقُولُواْ ٱشْهَدُواْ بِأَنَّا مُسْلِمُونَ ﴾ .

And also His Statement, Exalted is He: "Say: 'O People of the Scripture! Come to a word that is just, between us and you: That we do not worship anyone other than Allah, that we do not associate any partner with Him, and that we do not take each other as lords beside Allah.' If they turn away, then say: 'Bear witness that we are Muslims.'" [3:64]

POINT 50

TESTIFYING TO THE MESSENGERSHIP OF MUHAMMAD

وَدَلِيلُ شَهَادَةِ أَنَّ مُحَمَّدًا رَسُولُ اللهِ قَوْلُهُ تَعَالَى: ﴿لَقَدْ جَاءَكُمْ رَسُولٌ مِّنْ أَنفُسِكُمْ عَزِيزٌ عَلَيْهِ مَا عَنِتُّمْ حَرِيصٌ عَلَيْكُم بِالْمُؤْمِنِينَ رَءُوفٌ رَّحِيمٌ ﴾.

The proof for the testimony of Muhammad being the Messenger of Allah is His Statement, Exalted is He: "Certainly, a Messenger has come to you from your own selves. It grieves him when you face injury or difficulty. Devoutly concerned for you, he is kind and merciful toward the believers." [9:128]

THE MEANING OF THE TESTIMONY TO HIS MESSENGERSHIP

وَمَعْنَى شَهَادَةِ أَنَّ مُحَمَّدًا رَسُولُ اللهِ: طَاعَتُهُ فِيمَا أَمَرَ، وَتَصْدِيقُهُ فِيمَا أَخْبَرَ،
وَاجْتِنَابُ مَا عَنْهُ نَهَى وَزَجَرَ، وَأَنْ لَا يُعْبَدَ اللهُ إِلَّا بِمَا شَرَعَ.

And the meaning of the testimony that Muhammad is the Messenger of Allah is: [1] Obedience to him regarding what he has ordered. [2] Believing him regarding all that he has reported, [3] refraining from what he forbade and prohibited, and [4] that Allah is not worshipped except according to what he legislated.

POINT 52

THE UPRIGHT RELIGION OF TOWHEED, PRAYER, & ZAKAAT

وَدَلِيلُ الصَّلَاةِ وَالزَّكَاةِ وَتَفْسِيرُ التَّوْحِيدِ قَوْلُهُ تَعَالَى: ﴿وَمَآ أُمِرُوٓاْ إِلَّا لِيَعْبُدُواْ ٱللَّهَ مُخْلِصِينَ لَهُ ٱلدِّينَ حُنَفَآءَ وَيُقِيمُواْ ٱلصَّلَوٰةَ وَيُؤْتُواْ ٱلزَّكَوٰةَ وَذَٰلِكَ دِينُ ٱلْقَيِّمَةِ﴾.

The proof for prayer, zakaat, and the explanation of towheed is His Statement, Exalted is He: "And they were never ordered with anything other than worshipping Allah, making the Religion sincerely for Him as people of Islamic monotheism, and that they establish prayers and pay zakaat. And that (alone) is the Religion of uprightness." [98:5]

POINT 53

FASTING IS AN ACT OF WORSHIP

وَدَلِيلُ الصِّيَامِ قَوْلُهُ تَعَالَى: ﴿يَٰٓأَيُّهَا ٱلَّذِينَ ءَامَنُوا۟ كُتِبَ عَلَيْكُمُ ٱلصِّيَامُ كَمَا كُتِبَ عَلَى ٱلَّذِينَ مِن قَبْلِكُمْ لَعَلَّكُمْ تَتَّقُونَ﴾.

And the proof for fasting (as an act of worship) is the Statement of Allah, Exalted is He: "O you who believe! Fasting has been prescribed upon you as it was prescribed upon those before you, in order for you to attain piety." [2:183]

POINT 54

Hajj (Pilgrimage): an Act of Worship

وَدَلِيلُ الْحَجِّ قَوْلُهُ تَعَالَى : ﴿وَلِلَّهِ عَلَى ٱلنَّاسِ حِجُّ ٱلْبَيْتِ مَنِ ٱسْتَطَاعَ إِلَيْهِ سَبِيلًا وَمَن كَفَرَ فَإِنَّ ٱللَّهَ غَنِيٌّ عَنِ ٱلْعَٰلَمِينَ﴾ .

The proof for Hajj (as an act of worship) is His Statement, Exalted is He: "And due unto Allah is (a duty) upon the people: Pilgrimage to the House for whomsoever can find a way. Yet whoever disbelieves, verily Allah is free of any need from the Creation." [3:97]

POINT 55

THE SECOND LEVEL OF THE RELIGION: EEMAAN

المَرْتَبَةُ الثَّانِيَةُ: الإِيْمَانُ، وَهُوَ بِضْعٌ وَسَبْعُونَ شُعْبَةً، فَأَعْلَاهَا قَوْلُ لَا إِلَهَ إِلَّا اللهُ، وَأَدْنَاهَا إِمَاطَةُ الأَذَى عَنِ الطَّرِيقِ، وَالحَيَاءُ شُعْبَةٌ مِنَ الإِيْمَانِ.

The second level (of the Religion) is Eemaan (faith), which is seventy-some branches. The highest of which is the statement that none deserve worship other than Allah. The lowest of which is removing a harm from the road. And shyness is a branch of Eemaan.

POINT 56

THE SIX PILLARS OF EEMAAN (FAITH)

وَأَرْكَانُهُ سِتَّةٌ: أَنْ تُؤْمِنَ بِاللهِ، وَمَلَائِكَتِهِ، وَكُتُبِهِ، وَرُسُلِهِ، وَالْيَوْمِ الآخِرِ، وَبِالقَدْرِ خَيْرِهِ وَشَرِّهِ.

Its pillars are six: That you believe in [1] Allah, [2] His Angels, [3] His Books, [4] His Messengers, [5] the Last Day, and [6] Qadar, the good and bad of it.

POINT 57

FIVE PILLARS OF EEMAAN IN A QURANIC VERSE

وَالدَّلِيلُ عَلَى هَذِهِ الأَرْكَانِ السِّتَّةِ قَوْلُهُ تَعَالَى: ﴿لَّيْسَ ٱلْبِرَّ أَن تُوَلُّوا۟ وُجُوهَكُمْ قِبَلَ ٱلْمَشْرِقِ وَٱلْمَغْرِبِ وَلَـٰكِنَّ ٱلْبِرَّ مَنْ ءَامَنَ بِٱللَّهِ وَٱلْيَوْمِ ٱلْأَخِرِ وَٱلْمَلَـٰٓئِكَةِ وَٱلْكِتَـٰبِ وَٱلنَّبِيِّـۧنَ﴾.

The proof for these six pillars is His Statement, Exalted is He: "Piety is not (merely) that you turn your faces toward the East or the West. Rather, piety is believing in Allah, the Last Day, the Angels, the Books, and the Prophets." [2:177]

POINT 58

BELIEF IN QADAR, THE SIXTH PILLAR OF EEMAAN

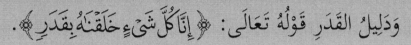

وَدَلِيلُ القَدَرِ قَوْلُهُ تَعَالَى: ﴿ إِنَّا كُلَّ شَيْءٍ خَلَقْنَاهُ بِقَدَرٍ ﴾.

The proof for Qadar is His Statement, Exalted is He:
"Verily, We have created all things by Qadar." [54:49]

POINT 59

THE ONE SINGULAR PILLAR OF IHSAAN

الْمَرْتَبَةُ الثَّالِثَةُ: الْإِحْسَانُ، رُكْنٌ وَاحِدٌ، وَهُوَ أَنْ تَعْبُدَ اللهَ كَأَنَّكَ تَرَاهُ،

فَإِنْ لَمْ تَكُنْ تَرَاهُ، فَإِنَّهُ يَرَاكَ.

The third level (of the Religion) is Ihsaan, a singular pillar, which is that you worship Allah as if you see Him; when you do not actually see Him, then (you know) He does see you.

POINT 60

ALLAH IS WITH THE PEOPLE OF IHSAAN

وَالدَّلِيلُ قَوْلُهُ تَعَالَى : ﴿ إِنَّ ٱللَّهَ مَعَ ٱلَّذِينَ ٱتَّقَوا۟ وَّٱلَّذِينَ هُم مُّحْسِنُونَ ﴾.

The proof (for Ihsaan) is His Statement, Exalted is He: "Verily, Allah is with those who are pious and those who are Muhsinoon (people of Ihsaan)." [16:128]

POINT 61

THE ALL-SEEING, ALL-HEARING, ALL-KNOWING

وَقَوْلُهُ تَعَالَى : ﴿وَتَوَكَّلْ عَلَى ٱلْعَزِيزِ ٱلرَّحِيمِ ۝ ٱلَّذِى يَرَىٰكَ حِينَ تَقُومُ ۝

وَتَقَلُّبَكَ فِى ٱلسَّٰجِدِينَ ۝ إِنَّهُۥ هُوَ ٱلسَّمِيعُ ٱلْعَلِيمُ ۝﴾ .

And His Statement, Exalted is He: "And place your trust in the All-Mighty, the Ever Merciful, the One who sees you whenever you stand (for prayer), and (He sees) your movements among those who prostrate. Verily, He is the All-Hearing, the All-Knowing." [26:217-220]

POINT 62

ALLAH WITNESSES WHATEVER WE DO, ALWAYS

وَقَوْلُهُ تَعَالَى: ﴿وَمَاتَكُونُ فِى شَأْنٍ وَمَاتَتْلُواْمِنْهُ مِن قُرْءَانٍ وَلَاتَعْمَلُونَ مِنْ عَمَلٍ إِلَّاكُنَّاعَلَيْكُمْ شُهُودًا إِذْ تُفِيضُونَ فِيهِ﴾.

And His Statement, Exalted is He: "Whatever situation you are in, whatever you recite of the Quran, no action would you ever perform, except that We are over you as Witness, at the time you are doing it." [10:61]

POINT 63

THE HADEETH OF JIBREEL (PART ONE)

وَالدَّلِيلُ مِنَ السُّنَّةِ حَدِيثُ جِبْرِيلَ المَشْهُورُ عَنْ عُمَرَ بْنِ الخَطَّابِ رَضِيَ اللهُ عَنْهُ قَالَ:
بَيْنَمَا نَحْنُ جُلُوسٌ عِنْدَ النَّبِيِّ صَلَّى اللهُ عَلَيْهِ وَسَلَّمَ إِذْ طَلَعَ عَلَيْنَا رَجُلٌ شَدِيدُ بَيَاضِ
الثِّيَابِ، شَدِيدُ سَوَادِ الشَّعْرِ، لَا يُرَى عَلَيْهِ أَثَرُ السَّفَرِ، وَلَا يَعْرِفُهُ مِنَّا أَحَدٌ، فَجَلَسَ إِلَى
النَّبِيِّ صَلَّى اللهُ عَلَيْهِ وَسَلَّمَ فَأَسْنَدَ رُكْبَتَيْهِ إِلَى رُكْبَتَيْهِ، وَوَضَعَ كَفَّيْهِ عَلَى فَخِذَيْهِ...

The proof (for Ihsaan) from the Sunnah is the hadeeth of Jibreel: Narrated by 'Umar ibn al-Khattaab –may Allah be pleased with him-, who said: "We were sitting with the Prophet –may Allah raise his rank and grant him peace-, when a man suddenly came to us, with very white garments and very black hair. No evidence of traveling could be seen upon him, nor were any of us familiar with him. He sat right up to the Prophet -may Allah raise his rank and grant him peace-, connecting his knees right up to his knees, placing his palms upon his thighs..."

POINT 64

The Hadeeth of Jibreel (Part Two)

...وَقَالَ: يَا مُحَمَّدُ! أَخْبِرْنِي عَنِ الإِسْلَامِ. قَالَ: «أَنْ تَشْهَدَ أَنْ لَا إِلَهَ إِلَّا اللهُ، وَأَنَّ مُحَمَّدًا رَسُولُ اللهِ، وَتُقِيمَ الصَّلَاةَ، وَتُؤْتِيَ الزَّكَاةَ، وَتَصُومَ رَمَضَانَ، وَتَحُجَّ البَيْتَ إِنِ اسْتَطَعْتَ إِلَيْهِ سَبِيلًا.» قَالَ صَدَقْتَ! فَعَجِبْنَا لَهُ يَسْأَلُهُ وَيُصَدِّقُهُ...

"...He said, 'O Muhammad! Tell me about Islam.' He replied, 'That you testify that no one has the right to be worshipped other than Allah and that Muhammad is the Messenger of Allah, establish prayers, pay zakaat, fast Ramadhaan, and make Hajj to the House if you are able to find a way.' He said, "You have spoken truthfully.' We were astonished at him, how he would ask him and then verify his answer as truthful!..."

POINT 65

THE HADEETH OF JIBREEL (PART THREE)

قَالَ: أَخْبِرْنِي عَنِ الإِيْمَانِ. قَالَ: «أَنْ تُؤْمِنَ بِاللهِ، وَمَلَائِكَتِهِ، وَكُتُبِهِ، وَرُسُلِهِ، وَالْيَوْمِ الآخِرِ، وَبِالْقَدَرِ خَيْرِهِ وَشَرِّهِ»...

"...He said, 'Tell me about Eemaan.' He replied, 'That you believe in Allah, His Angels, His Books, His Messengers, the Last Day, and the Qadar, the good and bad of it...'"

POINT 66

THE HADEETH OF JIBREEL (PART FOUR)

...قَالَ: أَخْبِرْني عَنِ الإِحْسَانِ. قَالَ: «أَنْ تَعْبُدَ اللهَ كَأَنَّكَ تَرَاهُ،

فَإِن لَمْ تَكُنْ تَرَاهُ، فَإِنَّهُ يَرَاكَ»...

"...He said, 'Tell me about Ihsaan.' He replied, 'That you worship Allah as if
you see Him; when you do not see him, (you know) He does see you...'"

POINT 67

THE HADEETH OF JIBREEL (PART FIVE)

...قَالَ: أَخْبِرْني عَنِ السَّاعَةِ. قَالَ: «مَا المَسْؤُولُ عَنْهَا بِأَعْلَمَ مِنَ السَّائِلِ»...

"...He said, 'Tell me about the Hour.' He replied, 'The one being asked knows no more than the questioner...'"

POINT 68

THE HADEETH OF JIBREEL (PART SIX)

قَالَ: أَخْبِرْنِي عَنْ أَمَارَاتِهَا. قَالَ: «أَنْ تَلِدَ الْأَمَةُ رَبَّتَهَا، وَأَنْ تَرَى الْحُفَاةَ الْعُرَاةَ الْعَالَةَ رِعَاءَ الشَّاءِ يَتَطَاوَلُونَ فِي الْبُنْيَانِ»...

"...He said, 'Tell me about its signs.' He replied, 'When the female slave gives birth to her master, and when you see the barefoot, naked shepherds, impoverished herdsmen of sheep, competing with one another in constructing tall buildings...'"

POINT 69

The Hadeeth of Jibreel (Part Seven)

قَالَ: فَمَضَى، فَلَبِثْنَا مَلِيًّا. فَقَالَ: «يَا عُمَرُ! أَتَدْرُونَ مَنِ السَّائِلُ؟»

قُلْنَا: اللهُ وَرَسُولُهُ أَعْلَمُ. قَالَ: «هَذَا جِبْرِيلُ أَتَاكُمْ يُعَلِّمُكُمْ أَمْرَ دِينِكُمْ.»

...He ('Umar) said: "Then he left, and we remained for a time. Then he said, 'Umar, do you know who the questioner was?' We replied, 'Allah and His Messenger know best.' He said, 'It was Jibreel; he came to you to teach you the affair of your Religion.'"

POINT 70

THE THIRD OF THE THREE FUNDAMENTAL PRINCIPLES

الأَصْلُ الثَّالِثُ: مَعْرِفَةُ نَبِيِّكُمْ مُحَمَّدٍ صَلَّى اللهُ عَلَيْهِ وَسَلَّمَ، وَهُوَ مُحَمَّدُ بْنُ عَبْدِالله
ابْنِ عَبْدِالْمَطَّلِبِ بْنِ هَاشِمٍ، وَهَاشِمٌ مِنْ قُرَيْشٍ، وَقُرَيْشٌ مِنَ الْعَرَبِ، وَالْعَرَبُ مِنْ ذُرِّيَّةِ
إِسْمَاعِيلَ بْنِ إِبْرَاهِيمَ الْخَلِيلِ عَلَيْهِ وَعَلَى نَبِيِّنَا أَفْضَلُ الصَّلَاةِ وَالسَّلَامِ.

The third principle is knowing about your Prophet, Muhammad –may Allah raise his rank and grant him peace-. He was Muhammad, the son of 'Abdullah, the son of 'Abdul-Muttalib, the son of Haashim. Haashim was from the Quraysh Tribe, the Quraysh are from the Arabs, and the Arabs are from the descendants of Ismaa'eel, the son of Ibraaheem, al-Khaleel –may Allah raise his rank in the best way, and that of our Prophet, and may He grant them both peace-.

وَلَهُ مِنَ العُمُرِ ثَلَاثٌ وَسِتُّونَ سَنَةً، مِنْهَا أَرْبَعُونَ قَبْلَ النُّبُوَّةِ، وَثَلَاثٌ وَعِشْرُونَ نَبِيًّا رَسُولًا.

نُبِّئَ بِاقْرَأْ، وَأُرْسِلَ بِالمُدَّثِّرِ. وَبَلَدُهُ مَكَّةُ، بَعَثَهُ اللهُ بِالنِّذَارَةِ عَنِ الشِّرْكِ، وَيَدْعُو إِلَى التَّوْحِيدِ.

He lived a life of 63 years. 40 of those years were before prophethood; 23 were as a Prophet and Messenger. He was made a Prophet with (Soorah) Iqra', and he was made a Messenger with (Soorah) al-Muddath-thir. His homeland was Makkah. Allah sent him to warn against shirk and to call to towheed.

POINT 72

THE OPENING VERSES OF SOORAH AL-MUDDATH-THIR

وَالدَّلِيلُ قَوْلُهُ تَعَالَى: ﴿يَٰٓأَيُّهَا ٱلۡمُدَّثِّرُ ۝ قُمۡ فَأَنذِرۡ ۝ وَرَبَّكَ فَكَبِّرۡ ۝ وَثِيَابَكَ فَطَهِّرۡ ۝ وَٱلرُّجۡزَ فَٱهۡجُرۡ ۝ وَلَا تَمۡنُن تَسۡتَكۡثِرُ ۝ وَلِرَبِّكَ فَٱصۡبِرۡ ۝﴾، وَمَعۡنَى ﴿قُمۡ فَأَنذِرۡ﴾: يُنْذِرُ عَنِ الشِّرْكِ، وَيَدْعُو إِلَى التَّوْحِيدِ. ﴿وَرَبَّكَ فَكَبِّرۡ﴾: عَظِّمْهُ بِالتَّوْحِيدِ. ﴿وَثِيَابَكَ فَطَهِّرۡ﴾، أَيْ: طَهِّرْ أَعْمَالَكَ مِنَ الشِّرْكِ. ﴿وَٱلرُّجۡزَ فَٱهۡجُرۡ﴾: الرُّجْزُ الأَصْنَامُ، وَهَجْرُهَا: تَرْكُهَا وَأَهْلِهَا وَالبَرَاءَةُ مِنْهَا وَأَهْلِهَا.

The proof is His Statement, Exalted is He: "O you who is wrapped in garments! Arise and warn! Your Lord, proclaim His Greatness! Your garments, purify them! Rujz (idols), shun them all! And do not give gifts hoping for more (in return)! For your Lord, have patience!" [74:1-7] The meaning of "Arise and warn" is: Warn against shirk and invite to towheed. "Your Lord, proclaim His Greatness" means: Declare His Greatness through towheed. "Your garments, purify them" means: Purify your actions of shirk. "Rujz, shun them all," Rujz are idols, and shunning them means abandoning them and their people and declaring yourself free of them and their people.

POINT 73

THE MAKKAN YEARS PRIOR TO HIJRAH

أَخَذَ عَلَى هَذَا عَشْرَ سِنِينَ يَدْعُو إِلَى التَّوْحِيدِ، وَبَعْدَ العَشْرِ عُرِجَ بِهِ إِلَى السَّمَاءِ، وَفُرِضَتْ عَلَيْهِ الصَّلَوَاتُ الخَمْسُ، وَصَلَّى فِي مَكَّةَ ثَلَاثَ سِنِينَ. وَبَعْدَهَا أُمِرَ بِالهِجْرَةِ إِلَى المَدِينَةِ.

He spent ten years calling to towheed. After these ten, he was taken up to the heavens, and the five daily prayers were made obligatory upon him. He prayed (those) in Makkah for three more years. Then, he was ordered to emigrate (make Hijrah) to al-Madeenah.

POINT 74

Hijrah (Emigration) is a Religious Obligation

وَالهِجْرَةُ الاِنْتِقَالُ مِنْ بَلَدِ الشِّرْكِ إِلَى بَلَدِ الإِسْلَامِ. وَالهِجْرَةُ فَرِيضَةٌ عَلَى هَذِهِ الأُمَّةِ مِنْ بَلَدِ الشِّرْكِ إِلَى بَلَدِ الإِسْلَامِ، وَهِيَ بَاقِيَةٌ إِلَى أَنْ تَقُومَ السَّاعَةُ.

Hijrah (emigration) is to move from the lands of shirk to the lands of towheed. Hijrah is a religious obligation upon this Ummah, to leave the lands of shirk for the lands of towheed. It remains (a duty) all the way until the Hour is established.

وَالدَّلِيلُ قَوْلُهُ تَعَالَى : ﴿ إِنَّ ٱلَّذِينَ تَوَفَّىٰهُمُ ٱلْمَلَٰئِكَةُ ظَالِمِى أَنفُسِهِمْ قَالُوا۟ فِيمَ كُنتُمْ قَالُوا۟ كُنَّا مُسْتَضْعَفِينَ فِى ٱلْأَرْضِ قَالُوٓا۟ أَلَمْ تَكُنْ أَرْضُ ٱللَّهِ وَٰسِعَةً فَتُهَاجِرُوا۟ فِيهَا فَأُو۟لَٰٓئِكَ مَأْوَىٰهُمْ جَهَنَّمُ وَسَآءَتْ مَصِيرًا ۝ إِلَّا ٱلْمُسْتَضْعَفِينَ مِنَ ٱلرِّجَالِ وَٱلنِّسَآءِ وَٱلْوِلْدَٰنِ لَا يَسْتَطِيعُونَ حِيلَةً وَلَا يَهْتَدُونَ سَبِيلًا ۝ فَأُو۟لَٰٓئِكَ عَسَى ٱللَّهُ أَن يَعْفُوَ عَنْهُمْ وَكَانَ ٱللَّهُ عَفُوًّا غَفُورًا ﴾.

The proof is His Statement, Exalted is He: "Verily, those whose souls are taken by the Angels, self-oppressive, they say to them: 'What were you doing?' They claim, 'We were oppressed in the land.' They say, 'Was not Allah's earth spacious enough for you to emigrate elsewhere?' The abode of such people is Jahannam, what an evil destination! Exempted are the truly oppressed among men, women, and children who could not find the strength to emigrate nor locate its path. Such people will be excused by Allah, and Allah is Ever Excusing, All-Forgiving." [4:97-99]

POINT 76

ALLAH REMINDS THE BELIEVERS ABOUT HIJRAH

وَقَوْلُهُ تَعَالَى: ﴿يَعِبَادِيَ الَّذِينَ ءَامَنُوٓاْ إِنَّ أَرْضِى وَاسِعَةٌ فَإِيَّـٰىَ فَاعْبُدُونِ﴾.

قَالَ البَغَوِيُّ رَحِمَهُ اللهُ: سَبَبُ نُزُولِ هَذِهِ الآيَةِ فِي المُسْلِمِينَ الَّذِينَ فِي مَكَّةَ،

لَمْ يُهَاجِرُوا، نَادَاهُمُ اللهُ بِاسْمِ الإِيْمَانِ.

And also His Statement, Exalted is He: "O My servants who have believed! Verily, My earth is spacious. Unto Me alone, render your worship." [29:56] Al-Baghawee –may Allah have Mercy on him- said: This Verse was revealed about Muslims who had remained in Makkah, not emigrating (to al-Madeenah). Allah addressed them by their ascription to faith.

وَالدَّلِيلُ عَلَى الهِجْرَةِ مِنَ السُّنَّةِ قَوْلُهُ صَلَّى اللهُ عَلَيْهِ وَسَلَّمَ: لَا تَنْقَطِعُ الهِجْرَةُ حَتَّى تَنْقَطِعَ التَّوْبَةُ، وَلَا تَنْقَطِعُ التَّوْبَةُ حَتَّى تَطْلُعَ الشَّمْسُ مِنْ مَغْرِبِهَا.

The proof for Hijrah (as a religious duty) from the Sunnah is his statement –may Allah raise his rank and grant him peace-, "Hijrah shall not cease until (the chance for) repentance is over. Repentance does not cease until the Sun rises from its Western horizon."

POINT 78

THE MADANI PERIOD OF THE PROPHET'S MISSION

فَلَمَّا اسْتَقَرَّ فِي المَدِينَةِ أُمِرَ بِبَقِيَّةِ شَرَائِعِ الإِسْلَامِ، مِثْلِ الزَّكَاةِ، وَالصَّوْمِ، وَالحَجِّ، وَالأَذَانِ، وَالجِهَادِ، وَالأَمْرِ بِالمَعْرُوفِ، وَالنَّهْيِ عَنِ المُنْكَرِ، وَغَيْرِ ذَلِكَ مِنْ شَرَائِعِ الإِسْلَامِ. أَخَذَ عَلَى هَذَا عَشْرَ سِنِينَ.

After he settled in al-Madeenah, he as ordered with the remaining legislated duties of Islam, like: Zakaat, fasting, Hajj, the athaan, jihaad, enjoining good, forbidding evil, and other legislated duties in Islam. He then spent ten years on this.

وَتُوُفِّيَ صَلَوَاتُ اللهِ وَسَلَامُهُ عَلَيْهِ وَدِينُهُ بَاقٍ، وَهَذَا دِينُهُ، لَا خَيْرَ إِلَّا دَلَّ الْأُمَّةَ عَلَيْهِ،

وَلَا شَرَّ إِلَّا حَذَّرَهَا مِنْهُ. وَالْخَيْرُ الَّذِي دَلَّهَا عَلَيْهِ التَّوْحِيدُ وَجَمِيعُ مَا يُحِبُّهُ اللهُ

وَيَرْضَاهُ. وَالشَّرُّ الَّذِي حَذَّرَهَا مِنْهُ الشِّرْكُ وَجَمِيعُ مَا يَكْرَهُ اللهُ وَيَأْبَاهُ.

Then, his soul was taken –may Allah raise his rank and grant him peace-, while his Religion remains. This is his Religion. There is no good thing except that he guided his Ummah to it, and there is no evil except that he warned his Ummah of it. The good that he guided his Ummah to is towheed, along with all things that Allah loves and is pleased with. The evil that he warned his Ummah of is shirk, along with all things that Allah hates and rejects.

POINT 80

THE MESSAGE OF ISLAM IS FOR ALL PEOPLE

بَعَثَهُ اللهُ إِلَى النَّاسِ كَافَّةً، وَافْتَرَضَ طَاعَتَهُ عَلَى جَمِيعِ الثَّقَلَيْنِ الجِنِّ وَالإِنْسِ.
وَالدَّلِيلُ قَوْلُهُ تَعَالَى: ﴿قُلْ يَا أَيُّهَا النَّاسُ إِنِّي رَسُولُ اللَّهِ إِلَيْكُمْ جَمِيعًا﴾.

Allah sent him to all of Mankind, and He made obedience to him obligatory upon the two races – both Jinn and Mankind. The proof is His Statement, Exalted is He: "Say: O Mankind! Verily I am the Messenger of Allah (sent) to all of you!" [7:158]

THE PERFECTED RELIGION CHOSEN FOR HUMANITY

وَكَمَّلَ اللهُ بِهِ الدِّينَ، وَالدَّلِيلُ قَوْلُهُ تَعَالَى: ﴿ٱلۡيَوۡمَ أَكۡمَلۡتُ لَكُمۡ دِينَكُمۡ وَأَتۡمَمۡتُ عَلَيۡكُمۡ نِعۡمَتِي وَرَضِيتُ لَكُمُ ٱلۡإِسۡلَٰمَ دِينٗا﴾.

Allah has perfected the Religion by way of him. The proof is His Statement, Exalted is He: "On this day, I have perfected your Religion for you, completed My Favor upon you, and chosen Islam for you as your Religion." [5:3]

POINT 82

THE PROPHET'S DEATH FORETOLD IN THE QURAN

وَالدَّلِيلُ عَلَى مَوْتِهِ صَلَّى اللهُ عَلَيْهِ وَسَلَّمَ قَوْلُهُ تَعَالَى: ﴿إِنَّكَ مَيِّتٌ وَإِنَّهُم مَّيِّتُونَ ٣٠﴾

ثُمَّ إِنَّكُمْ يَوْمَ الْقِيَامَةِ عِندَ رَبِّكُمْ تَخْتَصِمُونَ ٣١﴾.

The proof of his death –may Allah raise his rank and grant him peace- is His Statement, Exalted is He: "Verily, you are (soon to be) dead. And verily, they are also (soon to be) dead. Then on the Day of Judgment you will be before your Lord in disputation." [39:30-31]

POINT 83

THE INEVITABLE RESURRECTION AFTER DEATH

وَالنَّاسُ إِذَا مَاتُوا يُبْعَثُونَ، وَالدَّلِيلُ قَوْلُهُ تَعَالَى: ﴿مِنْهَا خَلَقْنَاكُمْ وَفِيهَا نُعِيدُكُمْ
وَمِنْهَا نُخْرِجُكُمْ تَارَةً أُخْرَى﴾، وَقَوْلُهُ تَعَالَى: ﴿وَاللَّهُ أَنْبَتَكُمْ مِنَ الْأَرْضِ نَبَاتًا ۝
ثُمَّ يُعِيدُكُمْ فِيهَا وَيُخْرِجُكُمْ إِخْرَاجًا ۝﴾.

The people will all be resurrected after death. The proof is His Statement, Exalted is He: "From it (the earth) We created you, into it We return you, and from it We will bring you forth once again." [20:55] And His Statement, Exalted is He: "And Allah has brought you forth from the earth, and then He returns you into it, and then brings you out once more." [71:17-18]

POINT 84

THE RECOMPENSE AFTER RESURRECTION

وَبَعْدَ الْبَعْثِ مُحَاسَبُونَ وَمَجْزِيُّونَ بِأَعْمَالِهِمْ، وَالدَّلِيلُ قَوْلُهُ تَعَالَى: ﴿وَلِلَّهِ مَا فِي ٱلسَّمَٰوَٰتِ وَمَا فِي ٱلْأَرْضِ لِيَجْزِيَ ٱلَّذِينَ أَسَٰٓـُٔوا۟ بِمَا عَمِلُوا۟ وَيَجْزِيَ ٱلَّذِينَ أَحْسَنُوا۟ بِٱلْحُسْنَى﴾.

Then, after the Resurrection, they are brought to account and recompensed for their actions. The proof is His Statement, Exalted is He: "To Allah belongs all that is in the heavens and everything on earth, that He might requite those who did evil based on their deeds and reward those who did well with al-Husnaa (the Finest Reward)." [53:31]

وَمَنْ كَذَّبَ بِالْبَعْثِ كَفَرَ، وَالدَّلِيلُ قَوْلُهُ تَعَالَى: ﴿زَعَمَ الَّذِينَ كَفَرُوٓا أَن لَّن يُبْعَثُوا۟ قُلْ بَلَىٰ وَرَبِّى لَتُبْعَثُنَّ ثُمَّ لَتُنَبَّؤُنَّ بِمَا عَمِلْتُمْ وَذَٰلِكَ عَلَى اللَّهِ يَسِيرٌ﴾.

Whoever rejects belief in the Resurrection has disbelieved. The proof is His Statement, Exalted is He: "The people who disbelieve have assumed that they will not be resurrected. Say: No, I swear by my Lord, you shall certainly be resurrected, and then you shall certainly be informed of what you have done. And that is, for Allah, an easy thing." [64:7]

POINT 86

MESSENGERS OF GLAD TIDINGS AND WARNINGS

وَأَرْسَلَ اللهُ جَمِيعَ الرُّسُلِ مُبَشِّرِينَ وَمُنْذِرِينَ، وَالدَّلِيلُ قَوْلُهُ تَعَالَى: ﴿رُسُلًا مُبَشِّرِينَ وَمُنْذِرِينَ لِئَلَّا يَكُونَ لِلنَّاسِ عَلَى اللَّهِ حُجَّةٌ بَعْدَ الرُّسُلِ﴾.

Allah sent all Messengers as bearers of glad tidings and warners. The proof is His Statement, Exalted is He: "Messengers, bearers of glad tidings and warners, so the people would have no plea against Allah after (the coming of) the Messengers." [4:165]

POINT 87

THE FIRST AND LAST OF THE MESSENGERS

وَأَوَّلُهُمْ نُوْحٌ عَلَيْهِ السَّلَامُ، وَآخِرُهُمْ مُحَمَّدٌ صَلَّى اللهُ عَلَيْهِ وَسَلَّمَ، وَهُوَ خَاتَمُ النَّبِيِّيْنَ، وَالدَّلِيْلُ عَلَى أَنَّ أَوَّلَهُمْ نُوْحٌ قَوْلُهُ تَعَالَى: ﴿ إِنَّا أَوْحَيْنَا إِلَيْكَ كَمَا أَوْحَيْنَا إِلَى نُوحٍ وَالنَّبِيِّينَ مِنْ بَعْدِهِ ﴾.

The first of them was Nooh –may Allah's Peace be upon him-; the last of them was Muhammad –may Allah raise his rank and grant him peace-, and he was the seal of all Prophets. The proof that the first one was Nooh is His Statement, Exalted is He: "Verily, We have sent Revelation to you, as We sent Revelation to Nooh and the Prophets after him." [4:163]

POINT 88

THE SAME MESSAGE THROUGHOUT HISTORY

وَكُلُّ أُمَّةٍ بَعَثَ اللهُ إِلَيْهِمْ رَسُولًا مِنْ نُوحٍ إِلَى مُحَمَّدٍ، يَأْمُرُهُمْ بِعِبَادَةِ اللهِ وَحْدَهُ، وَيَنْهَاهُمْ عَنْ عِبَادَةِ الطَّاغُوتِ، وَالدَّلِيلُ قَوْلُهُ تَعَالَى: ﴿وَلَقَدْ بَعَثْنَا فِى كُلِّ أُمَّةٍ رَسُولًا أَنِ اعْبُدُوا اللَّهَ وَاجْتَنِبُوا الطَّاغُوتَ﴾، وَافْتَرَضَ اللهُ عَلَى جَمِيعِ العِبَادِ الكُفْرَ بِالطَّاغُوتِ وَالإِيْمَانَ بِاللهِ.

To every nation Allah sent a Messenger, from Nooh to Muhammad, ordering them with the worship of Allah alone and forbidding them from the worship of taaghoot (false deities). The proof is His Statement, Exalted is He: "Verily, We have sent among every nation a Messenger, (proclaiming) that you must worship Allah and shun false deities." [16:36] So He required all worshippers to disbelieve in taaghoot and to believe (only) in Allah.

POINT 89

Ibn al-Qayyim's Definition of Taaghoot

قَالَ ابْنُ القَيِّمِ رَحِمَهُ اللهُ تَعَالَى: مَعْنَى الطَّاغُوتِ مَا تَجَاوَزَ بِهِ العَبْدُ حَدَّهُ مِنْ مَعْبُودٍ، أَوْ مَتْبُوعٍ، أَوْ مُطَاعٍ.

Ibn al-Qayyim –may Allah, the Exalted, have Mercy on him- said: The meaning of taaghoot is anything which a person exceeds the limits of, be it an object of worship (directly), or a leader or authority figure (indirectly).

POINT 90

THE FIVE MAIN KINDS OF TAAGHOOT

وَالطَّوَاغِيتُ كَثِيرُونَ، وَرُؤُوسُهُمْ خَمْسَةٌ: إِبْلِيسُ لَعَنَهُ اللهُ، وَمَنْ عُبِدَ وَهُوَ رَاضٍ، وَمَنْ دَعَا النَّاسَ إِلَى عِبَادَةِ نَفْسِهِ، وَمَنِ ادَّعَى شَيْئًا مِنْ عِلْمِ الغَيْبِ، وَمَنْ حَكَمَ بِغَيْرِ مَا أَنْزَلَ اللهُ.

False objects of worship are many types. The main ones are five: [1] Iblees –the curse of Allah be upon him-, [2] anyone pleased with worship directed to him, [3] one who invites people to worship him, [4] one who claims to have knowledge of the Unseen, and [5] one who rules by other than what Allah sent down.

POINT 91

DISBELIEF IN ALL FALSE OBJECTS OF WORSHIP

وَالدَّلِيلُ قَوْلُهُ تَعَالَى: ﴿لَا إِكْرَاهَ فِي ٱلدِّينِ قَد تَّبَيَّنَ ٱلرُّشْدُ مِنَ ٱلْغَيِّ فَمَن يَكْفُرْ بِٱلطَّٰغُوتِ وَيُؤْمِنۢ بِٱللَّهِ فَقَدِ ٱسْتَمْسَكَ بِٱلْعُرْوَةِ ٱلْوُثْقَىٰ لَا ٱنفِصَامَ لَهَاۗ وَٱللَّهُ سَمِيعٌ عَلِيمٌ﴾.

وَهَذَا هُوَ مَعْنَى لَا إِلَهَ إِلَّا اللهُ.

The proof is His Statement, Exalted is He: "There is no compulsion in the Religion. The path of guidance has become distinctly clear from the path of misguidance. So whoever disbelieves in false objects of worship and believes in Allah (alone) has latched onto the firmest handhold that shall never break. And Allah is All-Hearing, All-Knowing." [2:256]

POINT 92

CONCLUDING WITH A TREMENDOUS HADEETH

وَفِي الحَدِيثِ: «رَأْسُ الأَمْرِ الإِسْلَامُ، وَعَمُودُهُ الصَّلَاةُ،
وَذِرْوَةُ سَنَامِهِ الجِهَادُ فِي سَبِيلِ اللهِ»، وَاللهُ أَعْلَمُ.

*And in the hadeeth: "The head of the affair is Islam. Its main pillar is prayer.
The peak of the matter is striving in the Way of Allah." And Allah knows best.*

APPENDIX I

The Complete Text of the English Translation

THE THREE FUNDAMENTAL PRINCIPLES & THEIR EVIDENCES

In the Name of Allah, the Most Merciful, the Ever Merciful:

Know –may Allah have Mercy on you- that it is incumbent upon us to learn four matters:

[1] The first one is knowledge, which is awareness of Allah, awareness of His Prophet, and awareness of the Religion of Islam, with proofs.

[2] The second one is acting by it.

[3] The third one is calling to it.

[4] The fourth one is being patient with the harms that come with that.

The proof is His Statement, Exalted is He: "In the Name of Allah, the Most Merciful, the Ever Merciful. By the passing of time, Mankind is indeed in a state of loss, except for those who believe, perform righteous deeds, admonish one another with the Truth, and admonish one another with patience." [103:1-3]

Ash-Shaafi'ee –may Allah, the Exalted, have Mercy on him- said: Had Allah not sent down any proof upon His Creation other than this Soorah, it would have sufficed them.

And al-Bukhaaree –may Allah, the Exalted, have Mercy on him- said: Chapter: Knowledge Precedes Statements and Actions; the Proof is His Statement, Exalted is He: "So have knowledge (O Muhammad) that there is no one worthy of worship other than Allah, and seek forgiveness for your sin." [47:19] He began with knowledge, before (mentioning) statements or actions.

Know –may Allah have Mercy on you- that it is incumbent upon every Muslim, male or female, to learn three of these matters and act upon them: Firstly, that Allah has created us, provided for us, and not left us without purpose. Instead, He has sent a Messenger to us; whoever obeys him goes to Paradise, and whoever disobeys him goes to the Fire.

The proof is His Statement, Exalted is He: "Verily We have sent to you a Messenger as a witness over you, just as We sent to Pharaoh a Messenger. Yet, Pharaoh disobeyed the Messenger, so We seized him with a severe punishment." [73:16]

The second one is that Allah is not pleased with any partners being associated with Him in worship, not even an Angel brought near, nor any Prophet sent forth as a Messenger.

The proof is His Statement, Exalted is He: "And verily the masaajid are for Allah [alone], so do not call upon anyone along with Allah." [72:18]

The third one is that whoever obeys the Messenger and singles out Allah [in worship] is not allowed to have a religious loyalty to anyone who staunchly opposes Allah and His Messenger, even if he were the closest of kin.

The proof is His Statement, Exalted is He: "You do not find any people who believe in Allah and the Last Day loving those who staunchly oppose Allah and His Messenger, even if they were their fathers, children, brothers, or close kin. For such people, He has written for faith to enter their hearts, and He has aided them with a Rooh (i.e. proofs and guidance) from Himself. He shall place them in gardens under which rivers flow, abiding therein forever. He is pleased with them, and they are pleased with Him. Such people are the Hizb (Party) of Allah. Nay, the Hizb of Allah are indeed the successful ones." [58:22]

Know –may Allah guide you to His obedience- that Haneefiyyah (pure Islamic monotheism), the Religion of Ibraaheem, is that you worship Allah alone, dedicating yourself in Religion to Him exclusively. That is what Allah has ordered all of Mankind with and created them for. He, the Exalted, has said: "And I have not created the Jinn nor Mankind except for them to worship Me (alone)." [51:56] And the meaning of "to worship" is: to single out [Allah].

The greatest of all things that Allah has ordered is towheed, which is to single out Allah with all acts of worship. And the greatest (i.e. most sinful) thing He has forbidden is shirk, which is to call upon other than Him. The proof is His Statement, Exalted is He: "Worship Allah (alone), and do not associate a single partner with Him." [4:36]

If you are asked: "What are the three principles which all of Mankind must have awareness of?" Then say: "The worshipper's awareness of his Lord, his Religion, and his Prophet, Muhammad –may Allah raise his rank and grant him peace-."

If you are asked: "Who is your Lord?" Then say: "My Lord is Allah, the One who has sustained me and the entire universe by His Blessings. He (Alone) is my object of worship; I have no object of worship other than Him."

The proof is His Statement, Exalted is He: "All praise is due to Allah, the Lord, Creator, and Sustainer of the 'Aalameen." [1:1] And everything besides Allah is [called] an 'aalam (a created thing), and I am one of that 'aalam.

If you are asked: "How do you know about your Lord?" Then say: "By way of His great signs and creation. From His great signs are the night, the day, the Sun, and the Moon. And from His creation are the seven heavens, the seven earths, all those within them, and all that is between them."

The proof is His Statement, Exalted is He: "And from His Signs are the night, the day, the Sun, and the Moon. Do not prostrate to the Sun or the Moon, but instead prostrate to the One who created them, if it is Him that you truly worship." [41:37]

And His Statement, Exalted is He: "Verily, your Lord is Allah, the One who created the heavens and the earth in six days; He then ascended above the Throne. He brings the night as a covering over the day, coming after it rapidly. The Sun, the Moon, and the stars are all placed in [our] service, by His Command. Nay, to Him (Alone) belong the Creation and the Command. Blessed is He, the Lord of all the 'Aalameen." [7:54]

The Lord is the only One worthy of worship; the proof is His Statement, Exalted is He: "O Mankind! Worship your Lord who has created you and all of those before you, so you might attain piety. [He is] The One who made the earth a place of comfort for you, and the sky as a canopy. And He sent down from the sky rainwater and brought forth harvests as provisions for you. So do not set up rivals unto Allah, whilst you have knowledge." [2:22] Ibn Katheer said, "The Creator of these things is the (only) One worthy of worship."

The various kinds of worship which Allah has ordered are like: Islam, Eemaan, and Ihsaan. And from them is: Supplication, fear, hope, trust, ambition, awe, humility, knowledge-based fear, repentance, seeking assistance, refuge, and relief, slaughtering (animals), vows, and other kinds of worship that Allah has ordered; all of that is for Allah (alone).

The proof is His Statement, Exalted is He: "And verily the masaajid are for Allah [alone], so do not call upon anyone along with Allah." [72:18]

Whoever directs any of that to other than Allah is a polytheist disbeliever. The proof is His Statement, Exalted is He: "And whosoever calls upon another deity besides Allah, for which he has no proof, his account will be with his Lord alone. Verily, the disbelievers are not successful." [23:117]

And in the hadeeth: "Supplication is the core of worship."

The proof is also His Statement, Exalted is He: "And your Lord has said: Call upon Me; I shall answer you. Verily, those who arrogantly refuse to worship Me shall enter the Hellfire, in humiliation." [40:60]

The proof for fear (as a form of worship) is His Statement, Exalted is He: "So do not fear them, but instead fear Me, if you are indeed believers." [3:175]

The proof for hope (as a form of worship) is His Statement, Exalted is He: "So whoever hopes for the meeting with his Lord, let him work righteous deeds and not associate any partner in the worship of his Lord." [18:110]

The proof for trust (as a form of worship) is His Statement, Exalted is He: "So upon Allah (alone) place your trust, if you are indeed believers." [10:84] "And whoever places his trust in Allah (alone), He will suffice him." [65:3]

The proof for awe and humility (as forms of worship) is His Statement, Exalted is He: "Verily, they had hastened into good actions and called upon Us out of hope and fearful awe, surrendering unto Us in humility." [21:90]

The evidence for knowledge-based fear (as a form of worship) is His Statement, Exalted is He: "So do not fear them, but instead fear Me..." [5:3]

The proof for repentance (as a form of worship) is His Statement, Exalted is He: "And repent to your Lord, and submit unto Him (alone), before the punishment comes to you, after which you would never be aided..." [39:54]

The proof for seeking assistance (as a form of worship) is His Statement, Exalted is He: "You Alone we worship; You Alone we seek help from." [1:4]

And in the hadeeth: "Whenever you seek help, seek the help of Allah."

The proof for seeking refuge (as a form of worship) is His Statement, Exalted is He: "Say: I seek refuge with the Lord of Mankind." [114:1]

The proof for seeking relief (as a form of worship) is His Statement, Exalted is He: "And (remember) when you were seeking relief from your Lord, and He responded to your request..." [8:9].

The proof for slaughtering (animals, as a form of worship) is His Statement, Exalted is He: "Say: Verily my prayer, my slaughtering (of sacrificial animals), my living, and my dying are all for Allah, the Lord of the 'Aalameen." [6:162]

And from the Sunnah: "The curse of Allah is upon anyone who slaughters (a sacrificial animal) for other than Allah."

The proof for taking vows (as a form of worship) is His Statement, Exalted is He: "They fulfill their vows, and they fear a day, the evil of which is widespread." [76:7]

The second principle is awareness of the Religion of Islam with proofs, which is submission to Allah with toweed, surrendering to Him with obedience, and absolving oneself entirely of shirk. And that is three levels: Islam, Eemaan, and Ihsaan; each level has its own pillars.

The pillars of Islam are five:

[1] The testimony that no one deserves worship other than Allah and that Muhammad is His Messenger

[2] The establishment of prayer

[3] The payment of zakaat

[4] The fasting of Ramadhaan

[5] Making Hajj to the sacred House of Allah

The proof for the testimony is His Statement, Exalted is He: "Allah testifies that none have the right to be worshipped other than Him, and the Angels (also testify), and the people of knowledge, maintaining (His Creation) with Justice. No one has the right to be worshipped but Him, the All-Mighty, the Ever Wise." [3:18]

And its meaning is: There is no object of worship by right, other than Allah Alone. "Laa-elaaha" is a negation of all things worshipped beside Allah; "ill-Allah" is an affirmation of Allah's Right to be worshipped, which He shares with no one, just as no one shares in His Dominion.

The explanation which clarifies that is His Statement, Exalted is He: "And [remember] when Ibraaheem said to his father and his tribe: 'I am free of all those you worship, except for the One who created me; He shall surely guide me.' And he made that a word remaining after him, in order for them to return (to it after straying)." [43:26]

And also His Statement, Exalted is He: "Say: 'O People of the Scripture! Come to a word that is just, between us and you: That we do not worship anyone other than Allah, that we do not associate any partner with Him, and that we do not take each other as lords beside Allah.' If they turn away, then say: 'Bear witness that we are Muslims.'" [3:64]

The proof for the testimony of Muhammad being the Messenger of Allah is His Statement, Exalted is He: "Certainly, a Messenger has come to you from your own selves. It grieves him when you face injury or difficulty. Devoutly concerned for you, he is kind and merciful toward the believers." [9:128]

And the meaning of the testimony that Muhammad is the Messenger of Allah is:

[1] Obedience to him regarding what he has ordered.

[2] Believing him regarding all that he has reported,

[3] Refraining from what he forbade and prohibited, and

[4] That Allah is not worshipped except according to what he legislated.

The proof for prayer, zakaat, and the explanation of towheed is His Statement, Exalted is He: "And they were never ordered with anything other than worshipping Allah, making the Religion sincerely for Him as people of Islamic monotheism, and that they establish prayers and pay zakaat. And that (alone) is the Religion of uprightness." [98:5]

And the proof for fasting (as an act of worship) is the Statement of Allah, Exalted is He: "O you who believe! Fasting has been prescribed upon you as it was prescribed upon those before you, in order for you to attain piety." [2:183]

The proof for Hajj (as an act of worship) is His Statement, Exalted is He: "And due unto Allah is (a duty) upon the people: Pilgrimage to the House, whomsoever can find a way. And whoever disbelieves, then verily Allah is free of any need from the Creation." [3:97]

The second level (of the Religion) is Eemaan (faith), which is seventy-some branches. The highest of which is the statement that none deserve worship other than Allah. The lowest of which is removing a harm from the road. And shyness is a branch of Eemaan.

Its pillars are six - That you believe in:

[1] Allah

[2] His Angels

[3] His Books

[4] His Messengers

[5] The Last Day

[6] Qadar, the good and bad of it.

The proof for these six pillars is His Statement, Exalted is He: "Piety is not (merely) that you turn your faces toward the East or the West. Rather, piety is believing in Allah, the Last Day, the Angels, the Books, and the Prophets." [2:177]

The proof for Qadar is His Statement, Exalted is He: "Verily, We have created all things by Qadar." [54:49]

The third level (of the Religion) is Ihsaan, a singular pillar, which is that you worship Allah as if you see Him; when you do not actually see Him, then (you know) He does see you.

The proof (for Ihsaan) is His Statement, Exalted is He: "Verily, Allah is with those who are pious and those who are Muhsinoon (people of Ihsaan)." [16:128]

And His Statement, Exalted is He: "And place your trust in the All-Mighty, the Ever Merciful, the One who sees you whenever you stand (for prayer), and (He sees) your movements among those who prostrate. Verily, He is the All-Hearing, the All-Knowing." [26:217-220]

And His Statement, Exalted is He: "Whatever situation you are in, whatever you recite of the Quran, no action would you ever perform, except that We are over you as Witness, at the time you are doing it." [10:61]

The proof (for Ihsaan) from the Sunnah is the hadeeth of Jibreel: Narrated by 'Umar ibn al-Khattaab –may Allah be pleased with him-, who said: "We were sitting with the Prophet –may Allah raise his rank and grant him peace-, when a man suddenly came to us, with very white garments and very black hair. No evidence of traveling could be seen upon him, nor were any of us familiar with him. He sat right up to the Prophet -may Allah raise his rank and grant him peace-, connecting his knees right up to his knees, placing his palms upon his thighs.

He said, 'O Muhammad! Tell me about Islam.'

He replied, 'That you testify that no one has the right to be worshipped other than Allah and that Muhammad is the Messenger of Allah, establish prayers, pay zakaat, fast Ramadhaan, and make Hajj to the House if you are able to find a way.'

He said, "You have spoken truthfully.' We were astonished at him, how he would ask him and then verify his answer as truthful!

He said, 'Tell me about Eemaan.'

He replied, 'That you believe in Allah, His Angels, His Books, His Messengers, the Last Day, and the Qadar, the good and bad of it.'

He said, 'Tell me about Ihsaan.'

He replied, 'That you worship Allah as if you see Him; when you do not see him, (you know) He does see you.'

He said, 'Tell me about the Hour.'

He replied, 'The one being asked knows no more than the questioner.'

He said, 'Tell me about its signs.'

He replied, 'When the female slave gives birth to her master, and when you see the barefoot, naked shepherds, impoverished herdsmen of sheep, competing with one another in constructing tall buildings.'

He ('Umar) said: "Then he left, and we remained for a time.

Then he said, 'Umar, do you know who the questioner was?'

We replied, 'Allah and His Messenger know best.'

He said, 'It was Jibreel; he came to you to teach you the affair of your Religion.'"

The third principle is knowing about your Prophet, Muhammad –may Allah raise his rank and grant him peace-. He was Muhammad, the son of 'Abdullah, the son of 'Abdul-Muttalib, the son of Haashim. Haashim was from the Quraysh Tribe, the Quraysh are from the Arabs, and the Arabs are from the descendants of Ismaa'eel, the son of Ibraaheem, al-Khaleel –may Allah raise his rank in the best way, and that of our Prophet, and may He grant them both peace-.

He lived a life of 63 years. 40 of those years were before prophethood; 23 were as a Prophet and Messenger. He was made a Prophet with (Soorah) Iqra', and he was made a Messenger with (Soorah) al-Muddath-thir. His homeland was Makkah. Allah sent him to warn against shirk and to call to towheed.

The proof is His Statement, Exalted is He: "O you who is wrapped in garments! Arise and warn! Your Lord, proclaim His Greatness! Your garments, purify them! Rujz (idols), shun them all! And do not give gifts hoping for more (in return)! For your Lord, have patience!" (74:1-7) The meaning of "Arise and warn" is: Warn against shirk and invite to towheed. "Your Lord, proclaim His Greatness" means: Declare His Greatness through towheed. "Your garments, purify them" means: Purify your actions of shirk. "Rujz, shun them all," Rujz are idols, and shunning them means abandoning them and their people and declaring yourself free of them and their people.

He spent ten years calling to towheed. After these ten, he was taken up to the heavens, and the five daily prayers were made obligatory upon him. He prayed (those) in Makkah for three more years. Then, he was ordered to emigrate (make Hijrah) to al-Madeenah.

Hijrah (emigration) is to move from the lands of shirk to the lands of towheed. Hijrah is a religious obligation upon this Ummah, to leave the lands of shirk for the lands of towheed. It remains (a duty) all the way until the Hour is established.

The proof is His Statement, Exalted is He: "Verily, those whose souls are taken by the Angels, self-oppressive, they say to them: 'What were you doing?' They claim, 'We were oppressed in the land.' They say, 'Was not Allah's earth spacious enough for you to emigrate elsewhere?' The abode of such people is Jahannam, what an evil destination! Exempted are the truly oppressed among men, women, and children who could not find the strength to emigrate nor locate its path. Such people will be excused by Allah, and Allah is Ever Excusing, All-Forgiving." [4:97-99]

And also His Statement, Exalted is He: "O My servants who have believed! Verily, My earth is spacious. Unto Me alone, render your worship." [29:56] Al-Baghawee –may Allah have Mercy on him- said: This Verse was revealed about Muslims who had remained in Makkah, not emigrating (to al-Madeenah). Allah addressed them by their ascription to faith.

The proof for Hijrah (as a religious duty) from the Sunnah is his statement –may Allah raise his rank and grant him peace-, "Hijrah shall not cease until (the chance for) repentance is over. Repentance does not cease until the Sun rises from its Western horizon."

After he settled in al-Madeenah, he as ordered with the remaining legislated duties of Islam, like: Zakaat, fasting, Hajj, the athaan, jihaad, enjoining good, forbidding evil, and other legislated duties in Islam. He then spent ten years on this.

Then, his soul was taken –may Allah raise his rank and grant him peace-, while his Religion remains. This is his Religion. There is no good thing except that he guided his Ummah to it, and there is no evil except that he warned his Ummah of it. The good that he guided his Ummah to is towheed, along with all things that Allah loves and is pleased with. The evil that he warned his Ummah of is shirk, along with all things that Allah hates and rejects.

Allah sent him to all of Mankind, and He made obedience to him obligatory upon the two races – both Jinn and Mankind. The proof is His Statement, Exalted is He: "Say: O Mankind! Verily I am the Messenger of Allah (sent) to all of you!" [7:158]

Allah has perfected the Religion by way of him. The proof is His Statement, Exalted is He: "On this day, I have perfected your Religion for you, completed My Favor upon you, and chosen Islam for you as your Religion." [5:3]

The proof of his death –may Allah raise his rank and grant him peace- is His Statement, Exalted is He: "Verily, you are (soon to be) dead. And verily, they are also (soon to be) dead. Then on the Day of Judgment you will be before your Lord in disputation." [39:30-31]

The people will all be resurrected after death. The proof is His Statement, Exalted is He: "From it (the earth) We created you, into it We return you, and from it We will bring you forth once again." [20:55] And His Statement, Exalted is He: "And Allah has brought you forth from the earth, and then He returns you into it, and then brings you out once more." [71:17-18]

Then, after the Resurrection, they are brought to account and recompensed for their actions. The proof is His Statement, Exalted is He: "To Allah belongs all that is in the heavens and everything on earth, that He might requite those who did evil based on their deeds and reward those who did well with al-Husnaa (the Finest Reward)." [53:31]

Whoever rejects belief in the Resurrection has disbelieved. The proof is His Statement, Exalted is He: "The people who disbelieve have assumed that they will not be resurrected. Say: No, I swear by my Lord, you shall certainly be resurrected, and then you shall certainly be informed of what you have done. And that is, for Allah, an easy thing." [64:7]

Allah sent all Messengers as bearers of glad tidings and warners. The proof is His Statement, Exalted is He: "Messengers, bearers of glad tidings and warners, so the people would have no plea against Allah after (the coming of) the Messengers." [4:165]

The first of them was Nooh –may Allah's Peace be upon him-; the last of them was Muhammad –may Allah raise his rank and grant him peace-, and he was the seal of all Prophets. The proof that the first one was Nooh is His Statement, Exalted is He: "Verily, We have sent Revelation to you, as We sent Revelation to Nooh and the Prophets after him." [4:163]

To every nation Allah sent a Messenger, from Nooh to Muhammad, ordering them with the worship of Allah alone and forbidding them from the worship of taaghoot (false deities). The proof is His Statement, Exalted is He: "Verily, We have sent among every nation a Messenger, (proclaiming) that you must worship Allah and shun false deities." [16:36] So He required all worshippers to disbelieve in taaghoot and to believe (only) in Allah.

Ibn al-Qayyim –may Allah, the Exalted, have Mercy on him- said: The meaning of taaghoot is anything which a person exceeds the limits of, be it an object of worship (directly), or a leader or authority figure (indirectly). False objects of worship are many types. The main ones are five:

   [1] Iblees –the curse of Allah be upon him-

   [2] Anyone pleased with worship directed to him

   [3] One who invites people to worship him

   [4] One who claims to have knowledge of the Unseen

   [5] One who rules by other than what Allah sent down

The proof is His Statement, Exalted is He: "There is no compulsion in the Religion. The path of guidance has become distinctly clear from the path of misguidance. So whoever disbelieves in false objects of worship and believes in Allah (alone) has latched onto the firmest handhold that shall never break. And Allah is All-Hearing, All-Knowing." [2:256]

And in the hadeeth: "The head of the affair is Islam. Its main pillar is prayer. The peak of the matter is striving in the Way of Allah." And Allah knows best.

وَالدَّلِيلُ قَوْلُهُ تَعَالَى: ﴿لَا إِكْرَاهَ فِي الدِّينِ قَد تَّبَيَّنَ الرُّشْدُ مِنَ الْغَيِّ فَمَن يَكْفُرْ بِالطَّاغُوتِ وَيُؤْمِن بِاللَّهِ فَقَدِ اسْتَمْسَكَ بِالْعُرْوَةِ الْوُثْقَىٰ لَا انفِصَامَ لَهَا وَاللَّهُ سَمِيعٌ عَلِيمٌ﴾، وَهَذَا هُوَ مَعْنَى لَا إِلَهَ إِلَّا اللهُ.

وَفِي الْحَدِيثِ: «رَأْسُ الأَمْرِ الإِسْلَامُ، وَعَمُودُهُ الصَّلَاةُ، وَذِرْوَةُ سَنَامِهِ الجِهَادُ فِي سَبِيلِ اللهِ».

وَاللهُ أَعْلَمُ.

NOTE: This is the end of the complete voweled Arabic text which reads from right to left, beginning on page 118.

وَكَمَّلَ اللهُ بِهِ الدِّينَ، وَالدَّلِيلُ قَوْلُهُ تَعَالَى: ﴿ٱلْيَوْمَ أَكْمَلْتُ لَكُمْ دِينَكُمْ وَأَتْمَمْتُ عَلَيْكُمْ نِعْمَتِي وَرَضِيتُ لَكُمُ ٱلْإِسْلَامَ دِينًا﴾ .

وَالدَّلِيلُ عَلَى مَوْتِهِ صَلَّى اللهُ عَلَيْهِ وَسَلَّمَ قَوْلُهُ تَعَالَى: ﴿إِنَّكَ مَيِّتٌ وَإِنَّهُم مَّيِّتُونَ ٣٠ ثُمَّ إِنَّكُمْ يَوْمَ ٱلْقِيَامَةِ عِندَ رَبِّكُمْ تَخْتَصِمُونَ ٣١﴾ .

وَالنَّاسُ إِذَا مَاتُوا يُبْعَثُونَ، وَالدَّلِيلُ قَوْلُهُ تَعَالَى: ﴿مِنْهَا خَلَقْنَاكُمْ وَفِيهَا نُعِيدُكُمْ وَمِنْهَا نُخْرِجُكُمْ تَارَةً أُخْرَىٰ﴾، وَقَوْلُهُ تَعَالَى: ﴿وَٱللَّهُ أَنبَتَكُم مِّنَ ٱلْأَرْضِ نَبَاتًا ١٧ ثُمَّ يُعِيدُكُمْ فِيهَا وَيُخْرِجُكُمْ إِخْرَاجًا ١٨﴾ .

وَبَعْدَ الْبَعْثِ مُحَاسَبُونَ وَمَجْزِيُّونَ بِأَعْمَالِهِمْ، وَالدَّلِيلُ قَوْلُهُ تَعَالَى: ﴿وَلِلَّهِ مَا فِي ٱلسَّمَاوَاتِ وَمَا فِي ٱلْأَرْضِ لِيَجْزِيَ ٱلَّذِينَ أَسَاءُوا بِمَا عَمِلُوا وَيَجْزِيَ ٱلَّذِينَ أَحْسَنُوا بِٱلْحُسْنَى﴾ .

وَمَنْ كَذَّبَ بِالْبَعْثِ كَفَرَ، وَالدَّلِيلُ قَوْلُهُ تَعَالَى: ﴿زَعَمَ ٱلَّذِينَ كَفَرُوا أَن لَّن يُبْعَثُوا قُلْ بَلَىٰ وَرَبِّي لَتُبْعَثُنَّ ثُمَّ لَتُنَبَّؤُنَّ بِمَا عَمِلْتُمْ وَذَٰلِكَ عَلَى ٱللَّهِ يَسِيرٌ﴾ .

وَأَرْسَلَ اللهُ جَمِيعَ الرُّسُلِ مُبَشِّرِينَ وَمُنْذِرِينَ، وَالدَّلِيلُ قَوْلُهُ تَعَالَى: ﴿رُّسُلًا مُّبَشِّرِينَ وَمُنذِرِينَ لِئَلَّا يَكُونَ لِلنَّاسِ عَلَى ٱللَّهِ حُجَّةٌ بَعْدَ ٱلرُّسُلِ﴾ .

وَأَوَّلُهُمْ نُوحٌ عَلَيْهِ السَّلَامُ، وَآخِرُهُمْ مُحَمَّدٌ صَلَّى اللهُ عَلَيْهِ وَسَلَّمَ، وَهُوَ خَاتَمُ النَّبِيِّينَ، وَالدَّلِيلُ عَلَى أَنَّ أَوَّلَهُمْ نُوحٌ قَوْلُهُ تَعَالَى: ﴿إِنَّا أَوْحَيْنَا إِلَيْكَ كَمَا أَوْحَيْنَا إِلَىٰ نُوحٍ وَٱلنَّبِيِّينَ مِنۢ بَعْدِهِ﴾ .

وَكُلُّ أُمَّةٍ بَعَثَ اللهُ إِلَيْهِمْ رَسُولًا مِنْ نُوحٍ إِلَى مُحَمَّدٍ، يَأْمُرُهُمْ بِعِبَادَةِ اللهِ وَحْدَهُ، وَيَنْهَاهُمْ عَنْ عِبَادَةِ الطَّاغُوتِ، وَالدَّلِيلُ قَوْلُهُ تَعَالَى: ﴿وَلَقَدْ بَعَثْنَا فِي كُلِّ أُمَّةٍ رَّسُولًا أَنِ ٱعْبُدُوا ٱللَّهَ وَٱجْتَنِبُوا ٱلطَّاغُوتَ﴾، وَافْتَرَضَ اللهُ عَلَى جَمِيعِ الْعِبَادِ الْكُفْرَ بِالطَّاغُوتِ وَالإِيمَانَ بِاللهِ.

قَالَ ابْنُ الْقَيِّمِ رَحِمَهُ اللهُ تَعَالَى: مَعْنَى الطَّاغُوتِ مَا تَجَاوَزَ بِهِ الْعَبْدُ حَدَّهُ مِنْ مَعْبُودٍ، أَوْ مَتْبُوعٍ، أَوْ مُطَاعٍ. وَالطَّوَاغِيتُ كَثِيرُونَ، وَرُؤُوسُهُمْ خَمْسَةٌ: إِبْلِيسُ لَعَنَهُ اللهُ، وَمَنْ عُبِدَ وَهُوَ رَاضٍ، وَمَنْ دَعَا النَّاسَ إِلَى عِبَادَةِ نَفْسِهِ، وَمَنِ ادَّعَى شَيْئًا مِنْ عِلْمِ الْغَيْبِ، وَمَنْ حَكَمَ بِغَيْرِ مَا أَنْزَلَ اللهُ.

وَالدَّلِيلُ قَوْلُهُ تَعَالَى: ﴿يَا أَيُّهَا الْمُدَّثِّرُ ١ قُمْ فَأَنذِرْ ٢ وَرَبَّكَ فَكَبِّرْ ٣ وَثِيَابَكَ فَطَهِّرْ ٤ وَالرُّجْزَ فَاهْجُرْ ٥ وَلَا تَمْنُن تَسْتَكْثِرُ ٦ وَلِرَبِّكَ فَاصْبِرْ ٧﴾، وَمَعْنَى ﴿قُمْ فَأَنذِرْ﴾: يُنْذِرُ عَنِ الشِّرْكِ، وَيَدْعُو إِلَى التَّوْحِيدِ. ﴿وَرَبَّكَ فَكَبِّرْ﴾: عَظِّمْهُ بِالتَّوْحِيدِ. ﴿وَثِيَابَكَ فَطَهِّرْ﴾، أَيْ: طَهِّرْ أَعْمَالَكَ مِنَ الشِّرْكِ. ﴿وَالرُّجْزَ فَاهْجُرْ﴾: الرُّجْزُ الأَصْنَامُ، وَهَجْرُهَا: تَرْكُهَا وَأَهْلِهَا وَالبَرَاءَةُ مِنْهَا وَأَهْلِهَا.

أَخَذَ عَلَى هَذَا عَشْرَ سِنِينَ يَدْعُو إِلَى التَّوْحِيدِ، وَبَعْدَ العَشْرِ عُرِجَ بِهِ إِلَى السَّمَاءِ، وَفُرِضَتْ عَلَيْهِ الصَّلَوَاتُ الخَمْسُ، وَصَلَّى فِي مَكَّةَ ثَلَاثَ سِنِينَ، وَبَعْدَهَا أُمِرَ بِالهِجْرَةِ إِلَى المَدِينَةِ. وَالهِجْرَةُ الِانْتِقَالُ مِنْ بَلَدِ الشِّرْكِ إِلَى بَلَدِ الإِسْلَامِ. وَالهِجْرَةُ فَرِيضَةٌ عَلَى هَذِهِ الأُمَّةِ مِنْ بَلَدِ الشِّرْكِ إِلَى بَلَدِ الإِسْلَامِ، وَهِيَ بَاقِيَةٌ إِلَى أَنْ تَقُومَ السَّاعَةُ. وَالدَّلِيلُ قَوْلُهُ تَعَالَى: ﴿إِنَّ الَّذِينَ تَوَفَّاهُمُ المَلَائِكَةُ ظَالِمِي أَنفُسِهِمْ قَالُوا فِيمَ كُنتُمْ قَالُوا كُنَّا مُسْتَضْعَفِينَ فِي الأَرْضِ قَالُوا أَلَمْ تَكُنْ أَرْضُ اللَّهِ وَاسِعَةً فَتُهَاجِرُوا فِيهَا فَأُولَٰئِكَ مَأْوَاهُمْ جَهَنَّمُ وَسَاءَتْ مَصِيرًا ٩٧ إِلَّا المُسْتَضْعَفِينَ مِنَ الرِّجَالِ وَالنِّسَاءِ وَالوِلْدَانِ لَا يَسْتَطِيعُونَ حِيلَةً وَلَا يَهْتَدُونَ سَبِيلًا ٩٨ فَأُولَٰئِكَ عَسَى اللَّهُ أَنْ يَعْفُوَ عَنْهُمْ وَكَانَ اللَّهُ عَفُوًّا غَفُورًا﴾، وَقَوْلُهُ تَعَالَى: ﴿يَا عِبَادِيَ الَّذِينَ آمَنُوا إِنَّ أَرْضِي وَاسِعَةٌ فَإِيَّايَ فَاعْبُدُونِ﴾. قَالَ البَغَوِيُّ رَحِمَهُ اللَّهُ: سَبَبُ نُزُولِ هَذِهِ الآيَةِ فِي المُسْلِمِينَ الَّذِينَ فِي مَكَّةَ، لَمْ يُهَاجِرُوا، نَادَاهُمُ اللَّهُ بِاسْمِ الإِيمَانِ.

وَالدَّلِيلُ عَلَى الهِجْرَةِ مِنَ السُّنَّةِ قَوْلُهُ صَلَّى اللَّهُ عَلَيْهِ وَسَلَّمَ: لَا تَنْقَطِعُ الهِجْرَةُ حَتَّى تَنْقَطِعَ التَّوْبَةُ، وَلَا تَنْقَطِعُ التَّوْبَةُ حَتَّى تَطْلُعَ الشَّمْسُ مِنْ مَغْرِبِهَا.

فَلَمَّا اسْتَقَرَّ فِي المَدِينَةِ أُمِرَ بِبَقِيَّةِ شَرَائِعِ الإِسْلَامِ، مِثْلِ الزَّكَاةِ، وَالصَّوْمِ، وَالحَجِّ، وَالأَذَانِ، وَالجِهَادِ، وَالأَمْرِ بِالمَعْرُوفِ، وَالنَّهْيِ عَنِ المُنْكَرِ، وَغَيْرِ ذَلِكَ مِنْ شَرَائِعِ الإِسْلَامِ. أَخَذَ عَلَى هَذَا عَشْرَ سِنِينَ. وَتُوُفِّيَ صَلَوَاتُ اللَّهِ وَسَلَامُهُ عَلَيْهِ وَدِينُهُ بَاقٍ، وَهَذَا دِينُهُ، لَا خَيْرَ إِلَّا دَلَّ الأُمَّةَ عَلَيْهِ، وَلَا شَرَّ إِلَّا حَذَّرَهَا مِنْهُ. وَالخَيْرُ الَّذِي دَلَّهَا عَلَيْهِ التَّوْحِيدُ وَجَمِيعُ مَا يُحِبُّهُ اللَّهُ وَيَرْضَاهُ. وَالشَّرُّ الَّذِي حَذَّرَهَا مِنْهُ الشِّرْكُ وَجَمِيعُ مَا يَكْرَهُ اللَّهُ وَيَأْبَاهُ.

بَعَثَهُ اللَّهُ إِلَى النَّاسِ كَافَّةً، وَافْتَرَضَ طَاعَتَهُ عَلَى جَمِيعِ الثَّقَلَيْنِ الجِنِّ وَالإِنْسِ. وَالدَّلِيلُ قَوْلُهُ تَعَالَى: ﴿قُلْ يَا أَيُّهَا النَّاسُ إِنِّي رَسُولُ اللَّهِ إِلَيْكُمْ جَمِيعًا﴾.

وَقَوْلُهُ تَعَالَى: ﴿وَمَا تَكُونُ فِي شَأْنٍ وَمَا تَتْلُو مِنْهُ مِن قُرْآنٍ وَلَا تَعْمَلُونَ مِنْ عَمَلٍ إِلَّا كُنَّا عَلَيْكُمْ شُهُودًا إِذْ تُفِيضُونَ فِيهِ﴾.

وَالدَّلِيلُ مِنَ السُّنَّةِ حَدِيثُ جِبْرِيلَ المَشْهُورُ عَنْ عُمَرَ بْنِ الخَطَّابِ رَضِيَ اللهُ عَنْهُ قَالَ: بَيْنَمَا نَحْنُ جُلُوسٌ عِنْدَ النَّبِيِّ صَلَّى اللهُ عَلَيْهِ وَسَلَّمَ إِذْ طَلَعَ عَلَيْنَا رَجُلٌ شَدِيدُ بَيَاضِ الثِّيَابِ، شَدِيدُ سَوَادِ الشَّعْرِ، لَا يُرَى عَلَيْهِ أَثَرُ السَّفَرِ، وَلَا يَعْرِفُهُ مِنَّا أَحَدٌ، فَجَلَسَ إِلَى النَّبِيِّ صَلَّى اللهُ عَلَيْهِ وَسَلَّمَ فَأَسْنَدَ رُكْبَتَيْهِ إِلَى رُكْبَتَيْهِ، وَوَضَعَ كَفَّيْهِ عَلَى فَخِذَيْهِ، وَقَالَ: يَا مُحَمَّدُ! أَخْبِرْنِي عَنِ الإِسْلَامِ. قَالَ: «أَنْ تَشْهَدَ أَنْ لَا إِلَهَ إِلَّا اللهُ، وَأَنَّ مُحَمَّدًا رَسُولُ اللهِ، وَتُقِيمَ الصَّلَاةَ، وَتُؤْتِيَ الزَّكَاةَ، وَتَصُومَ رَمَضَانَ، وَتَحُجَّ البَيْتَ إِنِ اسْتَطَعْتَ إِلَيْهِ سَبِيلًا.» قَالَ صَدَقْتَ! فَعَجِبْنَا لَهُ يَسْأَلُهُ وَيُصَدِّقُهُ. قَالَ: أَخْبِرْنِي عَنِ الإِيمَانِ. قَالَ: «أَنْ تُؤْمِنَ بِاللهِ، وَمَلَائِكَتِهِ، وَكُتُبِهِ، وَرُسُلِهِ، وَاليَوْمِ الآخِرِ، وَبِالقَدَرِ خَيْرِهِ وَشَرِّهِ.» قَالَ: أَخْبِرْنِي عَنِ الإِحْسَانِ. قَالَ: «أَنْ تَعْبُدَ اللهَ كَأَنَّكَ تَرَاهُ، فَإِنْ لَمْ تَكُنْ تَرَاهُ، فَإِنَّهُ يَرَاكَ.» قَالَ: أَخْبِرْنِي عَنِ السَّاعَةِ. قَالَ: «مَا المَسْؤُولُ عَنْهَا بِأَعْلَمَ مِنَ السَّائِلِ.» قَالَ: أَخْبِرْنِي عَنْ أَمَارَاتِهَا. قَالَ: «أَنْ تَلِدَ الأَمَةُ رَبَّتَهَا، وَأَنْ تَرَى الحُفَاةَ العُرَاةَ العَالَةَ رِعَاءَ الشَّاءِ يَتَطَاوَلُونَ فِي البُنْيَانِ.» قَالَ: فَمَضَى، فَلَبِثْنَا مَلِيًّا. فَقَالَ: «يَا عُمَرُ! أَتَدْرُونَ مَنِ السَّائِلُ؟» قُلْنَا: اللهُ وَرَسُولُهُ أَعْلَمُ. قَالَ: «هَذَا جِبْرِيلُ أَتَاكُمْ يُعَلِّمُكُمْ أَمْرَ دِينِكُمْ.»

الأَصْلُ الثَّالِثُ: مَعْرِفَةُ نَبِيِّكُمْ مُحَمَّدٍ صَلَّى اللهُ عَلَيْهِ وَسَلَّمَ، وَهُوَ مُحَمَّدُ بْنُ عَبْدِاللهِ بْنِ عَبْدِالمُطَّلِبِ بْنِ هَاشِمٍ، وَهَاشِمٌ مِنْ قُرَيْشٍ، وَقُرَيْشٌ مِنَ العَرَبِ، وَالعَرَبُ مِنْ ذُرِّيَّةِ إِسْمَاعِيلَ بْنِ إِبْرَاهِيمَ الخَلِيلِ عَلَيْهِ وَعَلَى نَبِيِّنَا أَفْضَلُ الصَّلَاةِ وَالسَّلَام.

وَلَهُ مِنَ العُمُرِ ثَلَاثٌ وَسِتُّونَ سَنَةً، مِنْهَا أَرْبَعُونَ قَبْلَ النُّبُوَّةِ، وَثَلَاثٌ وَعِشْرُونَ نَبِيًّا رَسُولًا. نُبِّئَ بِاقْرَأْ، وَأُرْسِلَ بِالمُدَّثِّرِ.

وَبَلَدُهُ مَكَّةُ، بَعَثَهُ اللهُ بِالنِّذَارَةِ عَنِ الشِّرْكِ، وَيَدْعُو إِلَى التَّوْحِيدِ.

وَدَلِيلُ شَهَادَةِ أَنَّ مُحَمَّدًا رَسُولُ اللهِ قَوْلُهُ تَعَالَى: ﴿لَقَدْ جَاءَكُمْ رَسُولٌ مِنْ أَنْفُسِكُمْ عَزِيزٌ عَلَيْهِ مَا عَنِتُّمْ حَرِيصٌ عَلَيْكُمْ بِالْمُؤْمِنِينَ رَءُوفٌ رَحِيمٌ﴾.

وَمَعْنَى شَهَادَةِ أَنَّ مُحَمَّدًا رَسُولُ اللهِ: طَاعَتُهُ فِيمَا أَمَرَ، وَتَصْدِيقُهُ فِيمَا أَخْبَرَ، وَاجْتِنَابُ مَا عَنْهُ نَهَى وَزَجَرَ، وَأَنْ لَا يُعْبَدَ اللهُ إِلَّا بِمَا شَرَعَ.

وَدَلِيلُ الصَّلَاةِ وَالزَّكَاةِ وَتَفْسِيرُ التَّوْحِيدِ قَوْلُهُ تَعَالَى: ﴿وَمَا أُمِرُوا إِلَّا لِيَعْبُدُوا اللهَ مُخْلِصِينَ لَهُ الدِّينَ حُنَفَاءَ وَيُقِيمُوا الصَّلَاةَ وَيُؤْتُوا الزَّكَاةَ وَذَلِكَ دِينُ الْقَيِّمَةِ﴾.

وَدَلِيلُ الصِّيَامِ قَوْلُهُ تَعَالَى: ﴿يَا أَيُّهَا الَّذِينَ آمَنُوا كُتِبَ عَلَيْكُمُ الصِّيَامُ كَمَا كُتِبَ عَلَى الَّذِينَ مِنْ قَبْلِكُمْ لَعَلَّكُمْ تَتَّقُونَ﴾.

وَدَلِيلُ الْحَجِّ قَوْلُهُ تَعَالَى: ﴿وَلِلَّهِ عَلَى النَّاسِ حِجُّ الْبَيْتِ مَنِ اسْتَطَاعَ إِلَيْهِ سَبِيلًا وَمَنْ كَفَرَ فَإِنَّ اللهَ غَنِيٌّ عَنِ الْعَالَمِينَ﴾.

الْمَرْتَبَةُ الثَّانِيَةُ: الْإِيمَانُ، وَهُوَ بِضْعٌ وَسَبْعُونَ شُعْبَةً، فَأَعْلَاهَا قَوْلُ لَا إِلَهَ إِلَّا اللهُ، وَأَدْنَاهَا إِمَاطَةُ الْأَذَى عَنِ الطَّرِيقِ، وَالْحَيَاءُ شُعْبَةٌ مِنَ الْإِيمَانِ.

وَأَرْكَانُهُ سِتَّةٌ: أَنْ تُؤْمِنَ بِاللهِ، وَمَلَائِكَتِهِ، وَكُتُبِهِ، وَرُسُلِهِ، وَالْيَوْمِ الْآخِرِ، وَبِالْقَدَرِ خَيْرِهِ وَشَرِّهِ.

وَالدَّلِيلُ عَلَى هَذِهِ الْأَرْكَانِ السِّتَّةِ قَوْلُهُ تَعَالَى: ﴿لَيْسَ الْبِرَّ أَنْ تُوَلُّوا وُجُوهَكُمْ قِبَلَ الْمَشْرِقِ وَالْمَغْرِبِ وَلَكِنَّ الْبِرَّ مَنْ آمَنَ بِاللهِ وَالْيَوْمِ الْآخِرِ وَالْمَلَائِكَةِ وَالْكِتَابِ وَالنَّبِيِّينَ﴾.

وَدَلِيلُ الْقَدَرِ قَوْلُهُ تَعَالَى: ﴿إِنَّا كُلَّ شَيْءٍ خَلَقْنَاهُ بِقَدَرٍ﴾.

الْمَرْتَبَةُ الثَّالِثَةُ: الْإِحْسَانُ، رُكْنٌ وَاحِدٌ، وَهُوَ أَنْ تَعْبُدَ اللهَ كَأَنَّكَ تَرَاهُ، فَإِنْ لَمْ تَكُنْ تَرَاهُ، فَإِنَّهُ يَرَاكَ. وَالدَّلِيلُ قَوْلُهُ تَعَالَى: ﴿إِنَّ اللهَ مَعَ الَّذِينَ اتَّقَوْا وَالَّذِينَ هُمْ مُحْسِنُونَ﴾، وَقَوْلُهُ تَعَالَى: ﴿وَتَوَكَّلْ عَلَى الْعَزِيزِ الرَّحِيمِ ۝ الَّذِي يَرَاكَ حِينَ تَقُومُ ۝ وَتَقَلُّبَكَ فِي السَّاجِدِينَ ۝ إِنَّهُ هُوَ السَّمِيعُ الْعَلِيمُ ۝﴾.

وَدَلِيلُ الِاسْتِعَانَةِ قَوْلُهُ تَعَالَى: ﴿إِيَّاكَ نَعْبُدُ وَإِيَّاكَ نَسْتَعِينُ﴾، وَفِي الْحَدِيثِ: «إِذَا اسْتَعَنْتَ فَاسْتَعِنْ بِاللهِ.»

وَدَلِيلُ الِاسْتِعَاذَةِ قَوْلُهُ تَعَالَى: ﴿قُلْ أَعُوذُ بِرَبِّ النَّاسِ﴾.

وَدَلِيلُ الِاسْتِغَاثَةِ قَوْلُهُ تَعَالَى: ﴿إِذْ تَسْتَغِيثُونَ رَبَّكُمْ فَاسْتَجَابَ لَكُمْ﴾، الْآيَةُ.

وَدَلِيلُ الذَّبْحِ قَوْلُهُ تَعَالَى: ﴿قُلْ إِنَّ صَلَاتِي وَنُسُكِي وَمَحْيَايَ وَمَمَاتِي لِلَّهِ رَبِّ الْعَالَمِينَ﴾، وَمِنَ السُّنَّةِ: «لَعَنَ اللهُ مَنْ ذَبَحَ لِغَيْرِ اللهِ.»

وَدَلِيلُ النَّذْرِ قَوْلُهُ تَعَالَى: ﴿يُوفُونَ بِالنَّذْرِ وَيَخَافُونَ يَوْمًا كَانَ شَرُّهُ مُسْتَطِيرًا﴾.

الْأَصْلُ الثَّانِي: مَعْرِفَةُ دِينِ الْإِسْلَامِ بِالْأَدِلَّةِ، وَهُوَ الِاسْتِسْلَامُ لِلَّهِ بِالتَّوْحِيدِ، وَالِانْقِيَادُ لَهُ بِالطَّاعَةِ، وَالْخُلُوصُ مِنَ الشِّرْكِ. وَهُوَ ثَلَاثُ مَرَاتِبَ: الْإِسْلَامُ، وَالْإِيمَانُ، وَالْإِحْسَانُ، وَكُلُّ مَرْتَبَةٍ لَهَا أَرْكَانٌ.

فَأَرْكَانُ الْإِسْلَامِ خَمْسَةٌ: شَهَادَةُ أَنْ لَا إِلَهَ إِلَّا اللهُ، وَأَنَّ مُحَمَّدًا رَسُولُ اللهِ، وَإِقَامُ الصَّلَاةِ، وَإِيتَاءُ الزَّكَاةِ، وَصَوْمُ رَمَضَانَ، وَحَجُّ بَيْتِ اللهِ الْحَرَامِ.

فَدَلِيلُ الشَّهَادَةِ قَوْلُهُ تَعَالَى: ﴿شَهِدَ اللَّهُ أَنَّهُ لَا إِلَهَ إِلَّا هُوَ وَالْمَلَائِكَةُ وَأُولُو الْعِلْمِ قَائِمًا بِالْقِسْطِ لَا إِلَهَ إِلَّا هُوَ الْعَزِيزُ الْحَكِيمُ﴾.

وَمَعْنَاهَا: لَا مَعْبُودَ بِحَقٍّ إِلَّا اللهُ وَحْدَهُ.

وَلَا إِلَهَ: نَافِيًا جَمِيعَ مَا يُعْبَدُ مِنْ دُونِ اللهِ؛ إِلَّا اللهُ: مُثْبِتًا الْعِبَادَةَ لِلَّهِ وَحْدَهُ لَا شَرِيكَ لَهُ فِي عِبَادَتِهِ، كَمَا أَنَّهُ لَيْسَ لَهُ شَرِيكٌ فِي مُلْكِهِ.

وَتَفْسِيرُهَا الَّذِي يُوَضِّحُهَا قَوْلُهُ تَعَالَى: ﴿وَإِذْ قَالَ إِبْرَاهِيمُ لِأَبِيهِ وَقَوْمِهِ إِنَّنِي بَرَاءٌ مِمَّا تَعْبُدُونَ ٢٦ إِلَّا الَّذِي فَطَرَنِي فَإِنَّهُ سَيَهْدِينِ ٢٧ وَجَعَلَهَا كَلِمَةً بَاقِيَةً فِي عَقِبِهِ لَعَلَّهُمْ يَرْجِعُونَ ٢٨﴾، وَقَوْلُهُ تَعَالَى: ﴿قُلْ يَا أَهْلَ الْكِتَابِ تَعَالَوْا إِلَى كَلِمَةٍ سَوَاءٍ بَيْنَنَا وَبَيْنَكُمْ أَلَّا نَعْبُدَ إِلَّا اللَّهَ وَلَا نُشْرِكَ بِهِ شَيْئًا وَلَا يَتَّخِذَ بَعْضُنَا بَعْضًا أَرْبَابًا مِنْ دُونِ اللَّهِ فَإِنْ تَوَلَّوْا فَقُولُوا اشْهَدُوا بِأَنَّا مُسْلِمُونَ﴾.

وَالرَّبُّ هُوَ المَعْبُودُ، وَالدَّلِيلُ قَوْلُهُ تَعَالَى: ﴿يَٰٓأَيُّهَا ٱلنَّاسُ ٱعْبُدُواْ رَبَّكُمُ ٱلَّذِى خَلَقَكُمْ وَٱلَّذِينَ مِن قَبْلِكُمْ لَعَلَّكُمْ تَتَّقُونَ ۝ ٱلَّذِى جَعَلَ لَكُمُ ٱلْأَرْضَ فِرَٰشًا وَٱلسَّمَآءَ بِنَآءً وَأَنزَلَ مِنَ ٱلسَّمَآءِ مَآءً فَأَخْرَجَ بِهِۦ مِنَ ٱلثَّمَرَٰتِ رِزْقًا لَّكُمْ فَلَا تَجْعَلُواْ لِلَّهِ أَندَادًا وَأَنتُمْ تَعْلَمُونَ ۝﴾. قَالَ ابْنُ كَثِيرٍ: الخَالِقُ لِهَذِهِ الأَشْيَاءِ هُوَ المُسْتَحِقُّ لِلْعِبَادَةِ.

وَأَنْوَاعُ العِبَادَةِ الَّتِي أَمَرَ اللهُ بِهَا مِثْلُ الإِسْلَامِ، وَالإِيمَانِ، وَالإِحْسَانِ، وَمِنْهُ الدُّعَاءُ، وَالخَوْفُ، وَالرَّجَاءُ، وَالتَّوَكُّلُ، وَالرَّغْبَةُ، وَالرَّهْبَةُ، وَالخَشْيَةُ، وَالخُشُوعُ، وَالإِنَابَةُ، وَالاسْتِعَانَةُ، وَالاسْتِعَاذَةُ، وَالاسْتِغَاثَةُ، وَالذَّبْحُ، وَالنَّذْرُ، وَغَيْرُ ذَلِكَ مِنَ العِبَادَةِ الَّتِي أَمَرَ اللهُ بِهَا، كُلُّهَا لِلَّهِ، وَالدَّلِيلُ قَوْلُهُ تَعَالَى: ﴿وَأَنَّ ٱلْمَسَٰجِدَ لِلَّهِ فَلَا تَدْعُواْ مَعَ ٱللَّهِ أَحَدًا﴾.

فَمَنْ صَرَفَ مِنْهَا شَيْئًا لِغَيْرِ اللهِ فَهُوَ مُشْرِكٌ كَافِرٌ، وَالدَّلِيلُ قَوْلُهُ تَعَالَى: ﴿وَمَن يَدْعُ مَعَ ٱللَّهِ إِلَٰهًا ءَاخَرَ لَا بُرْهَٰنَ لَهُۥ بِهِۦ فَإِنَّمَا حِسَابُهُۥ عِندَ رَبِّهِۦٓ إِنَّهُۥ لَا يُفْلِحُ ٱلْكَٰفِرُونَ﴾. وَفِي الحَدِيثِ: الدُّعَاءُ مُخُّ العِبَادَةِ. وَالدَّلِيلُ قَوْلُهُ تَعَالَى: ﴿وَقَالَ رَبُّكُمُ ٱدْعُونِىٓ أَسْتَجِبْ لَكُمْ إِنَّ ٱلَّذِينَ يَسْتَكْبِرُونَ عَنْ عِبَادَتِى سَيَدْخُلُونَ جَهَنَّمَ دَاخِرِينَ﴾.

وَدَلِيلُ الخَوْفِ قَوْلُهُ تَعَالَى: ﴿فَلَا تَخَافُوهُمْ وَخَافُونِ إِن كُنتُم مُّؤْمِنِينَ﴾.

وَدَلِيلُ الرَّجَاءِ قَوْلُهُ تَعَالَى: ﴿فَمَن كَانَ يَرْجُواْ لِقَآءَ رَبِّهِۦ فَلْيَعْمَلْ عَمَلًا صَٰلِحًا وَلَا يُشْرِكْ بِعِبَادَةِ رَبِّهِۦٓ أَحَدًا﴾.

وَدَلِيلُ التَّوَكُّلِ قَوْلُهُ تَعَالَى: ﴿وَعَلَى ٱللَّهِ فَتَوَكَّلُوٓاْ إِن كُنتُم مُّؤْمِنِينَ﴾؛ ﴿وَمَن يَتَوَكَّلْ عَلَى ٱللَّهِ فَهُوَ حَسْبُهُۥ﴾.

وَدَلِيلُ الرَّغْبَةِ وَالرَّهْبَةِ وَالخُشُوعِ قَوْلُهُ تَعَالَى: ﴿إِنَّهُمْ كَانُواْ يُسَٰرِعُونَ فِى ٱلْخَيْرَٰتِ وَيَدْعُونَنَا رَغَبًا وَرَهَبًا وَكَانُواْ لَنَا خَٰشِعِينَ﴾.

وَدَلِيلُ الخَشْيَةِ قَوْلُهُ تَعَالَى: ﴿فَلَا تَخْشَوْهُمْ وَٱخْشَوْنِ﴾، الآيَةُ.

وَدَلِيلُ الإِنَابَةِ قَوْلُهُ تَعَالَى: ﴿وَأَنِيبُوٓاْ إِلَىٰ رَبِّكُمْ وَأَسْلِمُواْ لَهُۥ مِن قَبْلِ أَن يَأْتِيَكُمُ ٱلْعَذَابُ ثُمَّ لَا تُنصَرُونَ﴾، الآيَةُ.

الثَّالِثَةُ: أَنَّ مَنْ أَطَاعَ الرَّسُولَ وَوَحَّدَ اللهَ لَا يَجُوزُ لَهُ مُوَالَاةُ مَنْ حَادَّ اللهَ وَرَسُولَهُ وَلَوْ كَانَ أَقْرَبَ قَرِيبٍ، وَالدَّلِيلُ قَوْلُهُ تَعَالَى: ﴿لَا تَجِدُ قَوْمًا يُؤْمِنُونَ بِاللَّهِ وَالْيَوْمِ الْآخِرِ يُوَادُّونَ مَنْ حَادَّ اللَّهَ وَرَسُولَهُ وَلَوْ كَانُوا ءَابَاءَهُمْ أَوْ أَبْنَاءَهُمْ أَوْ إِخْوَانَهُمْ أَوْ عَشِيرَتَهُمْ أُولَئِكَ كَتَبَ فِي قُلُوبِهِمُ الْإِيمَانَ وَأَيَّدَهُم بِرُوحٍ مِّنْهُ وَيُدْخِلُهُمْ جَنَّاتٍ تَجْرِي مِن تَحْتِهَا الْأَنْهَارُ خَالِدِينَ فِيهَا رَضِيَ اللَّهُ عَنْهُمْ وَرَضُوا عَنْهُ أُولَئِكَ حِزْبُ اللَّهِ أَلَا إِنَّ حِزْبَ اللَّهِ هُمُ الْمُفْلِحُونَ﴾.

اعْلَمْ أَرْشَدَكَ اللهُ لِطَاعَتِهِ: أَنَّ الْحَنِيفِيَّةَ مِلَّةَ إِبْرَاهِيمَ أَنْ تَعْبُدَ اللهَ وَحْدَهُ مُخْلِصًا لَهُ الدِّينَ، وَبِذَلِكَ أَمَرَ اللهُ جَمِيعَ النَّاسِ وَخَلَقَهُمْ لَهَا، قَالَ تَعَالَى: ﴿وَمَا خَلَقْتُ الْجِنَّ وَالْإِنسَ إِلَّا لِيَعْبُدُونِ﴾، وَمَعْنَى يَعْبُدُونَ: يُوَحِّدُونَ.

وَأَعْظَمُ مَا أَمَرَ اللهُ بِهِ: التَّوْحِيدُ، وَهُوَ إِفْرَادُ اللهِ بِالْعِبَادَةِ. وَأَعْظَمُ مَا نَهَى عَنْهُ: الشِّرْكُ، وَهُوَ دَعْوَةُ غَيْرِهِ مَعَهُ، وَالدَّلِيلُ قَوْلُهُ تَعَالَى: ﴿وَاعْبُدُوا اللَّهَ وَلَا تُشْرِكُوا بِهِ شَيْئًا﴾.

فَإِذَا قِيلَ لَكَ: مَا الْأُصُولُ الثَّلَاثَةُ الَّتِي يَجِبُ عَلَى الْإِنْسَانِ مَعْرِفَتُهَا؟ فَقُلْ: مَعْرِفَةُ الْعَبْدِ رَبَّهُ، وَدِينَهُ، وَنَبِيَّهُ مُحَمَّدًا صَلَّى اللهُ عَلَيْهِ وَسَلَّمَ.

فَإِذَا قِيلَ لَكَ: مَنْ رَبُّكَ؟ فَقُلْ: رَبِّيَ اللهُ الَّذِي رَبَّانِي وَرَبَّى جَمِيعَ الْعَالَمِينَ بِنِعْمَتِهِ، وَهُوَ مَعْبُودِي، لَيْسَ لِي مَعْبُودٌ سِوَاهُ. وَالدَّلِيلُ قَوْلُهُ تَعَالَى: ﴿الْحَمْدُ لِلَّهِ رَبِّ الْعَالَمِينَ﴾، وَكُلُّ مَا سِوَى اللهِ عَالَمٌ، وَأَنَا وَاحِدٌ مِنْ ذَلِكَ الْعَالَمِ.

فَإِذَا قِيلَ لَكَ: بِمَ عَرَفْتَ رَبَّكَ؟ فَقُلْ: بِآيَاتِهِ وَمَخْلُوقَاتِهِ. وَمِنْ آيَاتِهِ: اللَّيْلُ، وَالنَّهَارُ، وَالشَّمْسُ، وَالْقَمَرُ. وَمِنْ مَخْلُوقَاتِهِ: السَّمَاوَاتُ السَّبْعُ، وَالْأَرَضُونَ السَّبْعُ، وَمَنْ فِيهِنَّ، وَمَا بَيْنَهُمَا. وَالدَّلِيلُ قَوْلُهُ تَعَالَى: ﴿وَمِنْ آيَاتِهِ اللَّيْلُ وَالنَّهَارُ وَالشَّمْسُ وَالْقَمَرُ لَا تَسْجُدُوا لِلشَّمْسِ وَلَا لِلْقَمَرِ وَاسْجُدُوا لِلَّهِ الَّذِي خَلَقَهُنَّ إِن كُنتُمْ إِيَّاهُ تَعْبُدُونَ﴾، وَقَوْلُهُ تَعَالَى: ﴿إِنَّ رَبَّكُمُ اللَّهُ الَّذِي خَلَقَ السَّمَاوَاتِ وَالْأَرْضَ فِي سِتَّةِ أَيَّامٍ ثُمَّ اسْتَوَى عَلَى الْعَرْشِ يُغْشِي اللَّيْلَ النَّهَارَ يَطْلُبُهُ حَثِيثًا وَالشَّمْسَ وَالْقَمَرَ وَالنُّجُومَ مُسَخَّرَاتٍ بِأَمْرِهِ أَلَا لَهُ الْخَلْقُ وَالْأَمْرُ تَبَارَكَ اللَّهُ رَبُّ الْعَالَمِينَ﴾.

APPENDIX II
The Complete Arabic Text (Voweled)

بِسْمِ اللهِ الرَّحْمَنِ الرَّحِيمِ

اعْلَمْ رَحِمَكَ اللهُ أَنَّهُ يَجِبُ عَلَيْنَا تَعَلُّمُ أَرْبَعِ مَسَائِلَ: الْأُولَى الْعِلْمُ، وَهُوَ مَعْرِفَةُ اللهِ، وَمَعْرِفَةُ نَبِيِّهِ، وَمَعْرِفَةُ دِينِ الْإِسْلَامِ بِالْأَدِلَّةِ. الثَّانِيَةُ الْعَمَلُ بِهِ. الثَّالِثَةُ الدَّعْوَةُ إِلَيْهِ. الرَّابِعَةُ الصَّبْرُ عَلَى الْأَذَى فِيهِ.

وَالدَّلِيلُ قَوْلُهُ تَعَالَى: بِسْمِ اللهِ الرَّحْمَنِ الرَّحِيمِ، ﴿وَالْعَصْرِ ۝ إِنَّ الْإِنسَانَ لَفِى خُسْرٍ ۝ إِلَّا الَّذِينَ ءَامَنُوا وَعَمِلُوا الصَّالِحَاتِ وَتَوَاصَوْا بِالْحَقِّ وَتَوَاصَوْا بِالصَّبْرِ ۝﴾. قَالَ الشَّافِعِيُّ رَحِمَهُ اللهُ تَعَالَى: لَوْ مَا أَنْزَلَ اللهُ حُجَّةً عَلَى خَلْقِهِ إِلَّا هَذِهِ السُّورَةَ لَكَفَتْهُمْ.

وَقَالَ الْبُخَارِيُّ رَحِمَهُ اللهُ تَعَالَى: بَابُ الْعِلْمِ قَبْلَ الْقَوْلِ وَالْعَمَلِ، وَالدَّلِيلُ قَوْلُهُ تَعَالَى: ﴿فَاعْلَمْ أَنَّهُ لَا إِلَهَ إِلَّا اللهُ وَاسْتَغْفِرْ لِذَنبِكَ﴾، فَبَدَأَ بِالْعِلْمِ قَبْلَ الْقَوْلِ وَالْعَمَلِ.

اعْلَمْ رَحِمَكَ اللهُ أَنَّهُ يَجِبُ عَلَى كُلِّ مُسْلِمٍ وَمُسْلِمَةٍ تَعَلُّمُ ثَلَاثِ هَذِهِ الْمَسَائِلِ وَالْعَمَلُ بِهِنَّ:

الْأُولَى: أَنَّ اللهَ خَلَقَنَا وَرَزَقَنَا وَلَمْ يَتْرُكْنَا هَمَلًا، بَلْ أَرْسَلَ إِلَيْنَا رَسُولًا، فَمَنْ أَطَاعَهُ دَخَلَ الْجَنَّةَ، وَمَنْ عَصَاهُ دَخَلَ النَّارَ، وَالدَّلِيلُ قَوْلُهُ تَعَالَى: ﴿إِنَّا أَرْسَلْنَا إِلَيْكُمْ رَسُولًا شَاهِدًا عَلَيْكُمْ كَمَا أَرْسَلْنَا إِلَى فِرْعَوْنَ رَسُولًا ۝ فَعَصَى فِرْعَوْنُ الرَّسُولَ فَأَخَذْنَاهُ أَخْذًا وَبِيلًا ۝﴾.

الثَّانِيَةُ: أَنَّ اللهَ لَا يَرْضَى أَنْ يُشْرَكَ مَعَهُ فِي عِبَادَتِهِ أَحَدٌ، لَا مَلَكٌ مُقَرَّبٌ، وَلَا نَبِيٌّ مُرْسَلٌ، وَالدَّلِيلُ قَوْلُهُ تَعَالَى: ﴿وَأَنَّ الْمَسَاجِدَ لِلَّهِ فَلَا تَدْعُوا مَعَ اللهِ أَحَدًا﴾.

118

والدليل قوله تعالى: ﴿لَا إِكْرَاهَ فِي ٱلدِّينِ قَد تَّبَيَّنَ ٱلرُّشْدُ مِنَ ٱلْغَيِّ فَمَن يَكْفُرْ بِٱلطَّٰغُوتِ وَيُؤْمِنْ بِٱللَّهِ فَقَدِ ٱسْتَمْسَكَ بِٱلْعُرْوَةِ ٱلْوُثْقَىٰ لَا ٱنفِصَامَ لَهَاۗ وَٱللَّهُ سَمِيعٌ عَلِيمٌ﴾، وهذا هو معنى لا إله إلا الله.

وفي الحديث: رأس الأمر الإسلام، وعموده الصلاة، وذروة سنامه الجهاد في سبيل الله.

والله أعلم.

NOTE: This is the end of the complete unvoweled Arabic text
which reads from right to left, beginning on page 127.

وكمل الله به الدين، والدليل قوله تعالى: ﴿ٱلۡيَوۡمَ أَكۡمَلۡتُ لَكُمۡ دِينَكُمۡ وَأَتۡمَمۡتُ عَلَيۡكُمۡ نِعۡمَتِي وَرَضِيتُ لَكُمُ ٱلۡإِسۡلَٰمَ دِينٗا﴾.

والدليل على موته صلى الله عليه وسلم قوله تعالى: ﴿إِنَّكَ مَيِّتٞ وَإِنَّهُم مَّيِّتُونَ ٣٠ ثُمَّ إِنَّكُمۡ يَوۡمَ ٱلۡقِيَٰمَةِ عِندَ رَبِّكُمۡ تَخۡتَصِمُونَ ٣١﴾.

والناس إذا ماتوا يبعثون، والدليل قوله تعالى: ﴿۞مِنۡهَا خَلَقۡنَٰكُمۡ وَفِيهَا نُعِيدُكُمۡ وَمِنۡهَا نُخۡرِجُكُمۡ تَارَةً أُخۡرَىٰ﴾، وقوله تعالى: ﴿وَٱللَّهُ أَنۢبَتَكُم مِّنَ ٱلۡأَرۡضِ نَبَاتٗا ١٧ ثُمَّ يُعِيدُكُمۡ فِيهَا وَيُخۡرِجُكُمۡ إِخۡرَاجٗا ١٨﴾.

وبعد البعث محاسبون مجزيون بأعمالهم، والدليل قوله تعالى: ﴿وَلِلَّهِ مَا فِي ٱلسَّمَٰوَٰتِ وَمَا فِي ٱلۡأَرۡضِ لِيَجۡزِيَ ٱلَّذِينَ أَسَٰٓـُٔواْ بِمَا عَمِلُواْ وَيَجۡزِيَ ٱلَّذِينَ أَحۡسَنُواْ بِٱلۡحُسۡنَى﴾.

ومن كذب بالبعث كفر، والدليل قوله تعالى: ﴿زَعَمَ ٱلَّذِينَ كَفَرُوٓاْ أَن لَّن يُبۡعَثُواْ قُلۡ بَلَىٰ وَرَبِّي لَتُبۡعَثُنَّ ثُمَّ لَتُنَبَّؤُنَّ بِمَا عَمِلۡتُمۡ وَذَٰلِكَ عَلَى ٱللَّهِ يَسِيرٞ﴾.

وأرسل الله جميع الرسل مبشرين ومنذرين، والدليل قوله تعالى: ﴿رُّسُلٗا مُّبَشِّرِينَ وَمُنذِرِينَ لِئَلَّا يَكُونَ لِلنَّاسِ عَلَى ٱللَّهِ حُجَّةُۢ بَعۡدَ ٱلرُّسُلِ﴾.

وأولهم نوح عليه السلام، وآخرهم محمد صلى الله عليه وسلم، وهو خاتم النبيين، والدليل على أن أولهم نوح قوله تعالى: ﴿إِنَّآ أَوۡحَيۡنَآ إِلَيۡكَ كَمَآ أَوۡحَيۡنَآ إِلَىٰ نُوحٖ وَٱلنَّبِيِّـۧنَ مِنۢ بَعۡدِهِ﴾.

وكل أمة بعث الله إليهم رسولا من نوح إلى محمد، يأمرهم بعبادة الله وحده، وينهاهم عن عبادة الطاغوت، والدليل قوله تعالى: ﴿وَلَقَدۡ بَعَثۡنَا فِي كُلِّ أُمَّةٖ رَّسُولًا أَنِ ٱعۡبُدُواْ ٱللَّهَ وَٱجۡتَنِبُواْ ٱلطَّٰغُوتَ﴾، وافترض الله على جميع العباد الكفر بالطاغوت والإيمان بالله.

قال ابن القيم رحمه الله تعالى: معنى الطاغوت ما تجاوز به العبد حده من معبود، أو متبوع، أو مطاع. والطواغيت كثيرون، ورؤوسهم خمسة: إبليس لعنه الله، ومن عبد وهو راض، ومن دعا الناس إلى عبادة نفسه، ومن ادعى شيئا من علم الغيب، ومن حكم بغير ما أنزل الله.

والدليل قوله تعالى: ﴿يَٰٓأَيُّهَا ٱلۡمُدَّثِّرُ ١ قُمۡ فَأَنذِرۡ ٢ وَرَبَّكَ فَكَبِّرۡ ٣ وَثِيَابَكَ فَطَهِّرۡ ٤ وَٱلرُّجۡزَ فَٱهۡجُرۡ ٥ وَلَا تَمۡنُن تَسۡتَكۡثِرُ ٦ وَلِرَبِّكَ فَٱصۡبِرۡ ٧﴾، ومعنى ﴿قُمۡ فَأَنذِرۡ﴾: ينذر عن الشرك، ويدعو إلى التوحيد. ﴿وَرَبَّكَ فَكَبِّرۡ﴾: عظمه بالتوحيد. ﴿وَثِيَابَكَ فَطَهِّرۡ﴾، أي: طهر أعمالك من الشرك. ﴿وَٱلرُّجۡزَ فَٱهۡجُرۡ﴾: الرجز الأصنام، وهجرها: تركها وأهلها والبراءة منها وأهلها.

أخذ على هذا عشر سنين يدعو إلى التوحيد، وبعد العشر عرج به إلى السماء، وفرضت عليه الصلوات الخمس، وصلى في مكة ثلاث سنين، وبعدها أمر بالهجرة إلى المدينة. والهجرة الانتقال من بلد الشرك إلى بلد الإسلام. والهجرة فريضة على هذه الأمة من بلد الشرك إلى بلد الإسلام، وهي باقية إلى أن تقوم الساعة. والدليل قوله تعالى: ﴿إِنَّ ٱلَّذِينَ تَوَفَّىٰهُمُ ٱلۡمَلَٰٓئِكَةُ ظَالِمِيٓ أَنفُسِهِمۡ قَالُواْ فِيمَ كُنتُمۡۖ قَالُواْ كُنَّا مُسۡتَضۡعَفِينَ فِي ٱلۡأَرۡضِۚ قَالُوٓاْ أَلَمۡ تَكُنۡ أَرۡضُ ٱللَّهِ وَٰسِعَةٗ فَتُهَاجِرُواْ فِيهَاۚ فَأُوْلَٰٓئِكَ مَأۡوَىٰهُمۡ جَهَنَّمُۖ وَسَآءَتۡ مَصِيرًا ٩٧ إِلَّا ٱلۡمُسۡتَضۡعَفِينَ مِنَ ٱلرِّجَالِ وَٱلنِّسَآءِ وَٱلۡوِلۡدَٰنِ لَا يَسۡتَطِيعُونَ حِيلَةٗ وَلَا يَهۡتَدُونَ سَبِيلٗا ٩٨ فَأُوْلَٰٓئِكَ عَسَى ٱللَّهُ أَن يَعۡفُوَ عَنۡهُمۡۚ وَكَانَ ٱللَّهُ عَفُوًّا غَفُورٗا﴾، وقوله تعالى: ﴿يَٰعِبَادِيَ ٱلَّذِينَ ءَامَنُوٓاْ إِنَّ أَرۡضِي وَٰسِعَةٞ فَإِيَّٰيَ فَٱعۡبُدُونِ﴾. قال البغوي رحمه الله: سبب نزول هذه الآية في المسلمين الذين في مكة، لم يهاجروا، ناداهم الله باسم الإيمان.

والدليل على الهجرة من السنة قوله صلى الله عليه وسلم: لا تنقطع الهجرة حتى تنقطع التوبة، ولا تنقطع التوبة حتى تطلع الشمس من مغربها.

فلما استقر في المدينة أمر ببقية شرائع الإسلام، مثل الزكاة، والصوم، والحج، والأذان، والجهاد، والأمر بالمعروف، والنهي عن المنكر، وغير ذلك من شرائع الإسلام. أخذ على هذا عشر سنين. وتوفي صلوات الله وسلامه عليه ودينه باق، وهذا دينه، لا خير إلا دل الأمة عليه، ولا شر إلا حذرها منه. والخير الذي دلها عليه التوحيد وجميع ما يحبه الله ويرضاه. والشر الذي حذرها منه الشرك وجميع ما يكره الله ويأباه.

بعثه الله إلى الناس كافة، وافترض طاعته على جميع الثقلين الجن والإنس. والدليل قوله تعالى: ﴿قُلۡ يَٰٓأَيُّهَا ٱلنَّاسُ إِنِّي رَسُولُ ٱللَّهِ إِلَيۡكُمۡ جَمِيعًا﴾.

وقوله تعالى: ﴿ وَمَا تَكُونُ فِي شَأْنٍ وَمَا تَتْلُواْ مِنْهُ مِن قُرْءَانٍ وَلَا تَعْمَلُونَ مِنْ عَمَلٍ إِلَّا كُنَّا عَلَيْكُمْ شُهُودًا إِذْ تُفِيضُونَ فِيهِ ﴾.

والدليل من السنة حديث جبريل المشهور عن عمر بن الخطاب رضي الله عنه قال: بينما نحن جلوس عند النبي صلى الله عليه وسلم إذ طلع علينا رجل شديد بياض الثياب، شديد سواد الشعر، لا يرى عليه أثر السفر، ولا يعرفه منا أحد، فجلس إلى النبي صلى الله عليه وسلم فأسند ركبتيه إلى ركبتيه، ووضع كفيه على فخذيه، وقال: يا محمد! أخبرني عن الإسلام. قال: أن تشهد أن لا إله إلا الله، وأن محمدا رسول الله، وتقيم الصلاة، وتؤتي الزكاة، وتصوم رمضان، وتحج البيت إن استطعت إليه سبيلا. قال صدقت! فعجبنا له يسأله ويصدقه. قال: أخبرني عن الإيمان. قال: أن تؤمن بالله، وملائكته، وكتبه، ورسله، واليوم الآخر، وبالقدر خيره وشره. قال: أخبرني عن الإحسان. قال: أن تعبد الله كأنك تراه، فإن لم تكن تراه، فإنه يراك. قال: أخبرني عن الساعة. قال: ما المسؤول عنها بأعلم من السائل. قال: أخبرني عن أماراتها. قال: أن تلد الأمة ربتها، وأن ترى الحفاة العراة العالة رعاء الشاء يتطاولون في البنيان. قال: فمضى، فلبثنا مليا. فقال: يا عمر! أتدرون من السائل؟ قلنا: الله ورسوله أعلم. قال: هذا جبريل أتاكم يعلمكم أمر دينكم.

الأصل الثالث: معرفة نبيكم محمد صلى الله عليه وسلم، وهو محمد بن عبدالله بن عبدالمطلب بن هاشم، وهاشم من قريش، وقريش من العرب، والعرب من ذرية إسماعيل بن إبراهيم الخليل عليه وعلى نبينا أفضل الصلاة والسلام.

وله من العمر ثلاث وستون سنة، منها أربعون قبل النبوة، وثلاث وعشرون نبيا رسولا. نبئ باقرأ، وأرسل بالمدثر.

وبلده مكة، بعثه الله بالنذارة عن الشرك، ويدعو إلى التوحيد.

ودليل شهادة أن محمدا رسول الله قوله تعالى: ﴿لَقَدْ جَآءَكُمْ رَسُولٌ مِّنْ أَنفُسِكُمْ عَزِيزٌ عَلَيْهِ مَا عَنِتُّمْ حَرِيصٌ عَلَيْكُم بِالْمُؤْمِنِينَ رَءُوفٌ رَّحِيمٌ﴾.

ومعنى شهادة أن محمدا رسول الله: طاعته فيما أمر، وتصديقه فيما أخبر، واجتناب ما عنه نهى وزجر، وأن لا يعبد الله إلا بما شرع.

ودليل الصلاة والزكاة وتفسير التوحيد قوله تعالى: ﴿وَمَآ أُمِرُوٓا إِلَّا لِيَعْبُدُوا اللَّهَ مُخْلِصِينَ لَهُ الدِّينَ حُنَفَآءَ وَيُقِيمُوا الصَّلَوٰةَ وَيُؤْتُوا الزَّكَوٰةَ وَذَٰلِكَ دِينُ الْقَيِّمَةِ﴾.

ودليل الصيام قوله تعالى: ﴿يَٰٓأَيُّهَا الَّذِينَ ءَامَنُوا كُتِبَ عَلَيْكُمُ الصِّيَامُ كَمَا كُتِبَ عَلَى الَّذِينَ مِن قَبْلِكُمْ لَعَلَّكُمْ تَتَّقُونَ﴾.

ودليل الحج قوله تعالى: ﴿وَلِلَّهِ عَلَى النَّاسِ حِجُّ الْبَيْتِ مَنِ اسْتَطَاعَ إِلَيْهِ سَبِيلًا وَمَن كَفَرَ فَإِنَّ اللَّهَ غَنِيٌّ عَنِ الْعَالَمِينَ﴾.

المرتبة الثانية: الإيمان، وهو بضع وسبعون شعبة، فأعلاها قول لا إله إلا الله، وأدناها إماطة الأذى عن الطريق، والحياء شعبة من الإيمان.

وأركانه ستة: أن تؤمن بالله، وملائكته، وكتبه، ورسله، واليوم الآخر، وبالقدر خيره وشره.

والدليل على هذه الأركان الستة قوله تعالى: ﴿لَّيْسَ الْبِرَّ أَن تُوَلُّوا وُجُوهَكُمْ قِبَلَ الْمَشْرِقِ وَالْمَغْرِبِ وَلَٰكِنَّ الْبِرَّ مَنْ ءَامَنَ بِاللَّهِ وَالْيَوْمِ الْآخِرِ وَالْمَلَٰٓئِكَةِ وَالْكِتَٰبِ وَالنَّبِيِّۧنَ﴾.

ودليل القدر قوله تعالى: ﴿إِنَّا كُلَّ شَيْءٍ خَلَقْنَٰهُ بِقَدَرٍ﴾.

المرتبة الثالثة: الإحسان، ركن واحد، وهو أن تعبد الله كأنك تراه، فإن لم تكن تراه، فإنه يراك. والدليل قوله تعالى: ﴿إِنَّ اللَّهَ مَعَ الَّذِينَ اتَّقَوا وَّالَّذِينَ هُم مُّحْسِنُونَ﴾، وقوله تعالى: ﴿وَتَوَكَّلْ عَلَى الْعَزِيزِ الرَّحِيمِ ۝ الَّذِي يَرَاكَ حِينَ تَقُومُ ۝ وَتَقَلُّبَكَ فِي السَّاجِدِينَ ۝ إِنَّهُ هُوَ السَّمِيعُ الْعَلِيمُ ۝﴾.

ودليل الاستعانة قوله تعالى: ﴿إِيَّاكَ نَعْبُدُ وَإِيَّاكَ نَسْتَعِينُ﴾، وفي الحديث: «إذا استعنت فاستعن بالله.»

ودليل الاستعاذة قوله تعالى: ﴿قُلْ أَعُوذُ بِرَبِّ النَّاسِ﴾.

ودليل الاستغاثة قوله تعالى: ﴿إِذْ تَسْتَغِيثُونَ رَبَّكُمْ فَاسْتَجَابَ لَكُمْ﴾، الآية.

ودليل الذبح قوله تعالى: ﴿قُلْ إِنَّ صَلَاتِي وَنُسُكِي وَمَحْيَايَ وَمَمَاتِي لِلَّهِ رَبِّ الْعَالَمِينَ﴾، ومن السنة: «لعن الله من ذبح لغير الله.»

ودليل النذر قوله تعالى: ﴿يُوفُونَ بِالنَّذْرِ وَيَخَافُونَ يَوْمًا كَانَ شَرُّهُ مُسْتَطِيرًا﴾.

الأصل الثاني: معرفة دين الإسلام بالأدلة، وهو الاستسلام لله بالتوحيد، والانقياد له بالطاعة، والخلوص من الشرك. وهو ثلاث مراتب: الإسلام، والإيمان، والإحسان، وكل مرتبة لها أركان.

فأركان الإسلام خمسة: شهادة أن لا إله إلا الله، وأن محمدا رسول الله، وإقام الصلاة، وإيتاء الزكاة، وصوم رمضان، وحج بيت الله الحرام.

فدليل الشهادة قوله تعالى: ﴿شَهِدَ اللَّهُ أَنَّهُ لَا إِلَٰهَ إِلَّا هُوَ وَالْمَلَائِكَةُ وَأُولُو الْعِلْمِ قَائِمًا بِالْقِسْطِ لَا إِلَٰهَ إِلَّا هُوَ الْعَزِيزُ الْحَكِيمُ﴾.

ومعناها: لا معبود بحق إلا الله وحده؛

ولا إله: نافيا جميع ما يعبد من دون الله؛ إلا الله: مثبتا العبادة لله وحده لا شريك له في عبادته، كما أنه ليس له شريك في ملكه.

وتفسيرها الذي يوضحها قوله تعالى: ﴿وَإِذْ قَالَ إِبْرَاهِيمُ لِأَبِيهِ وَقَوْمِهِ إِنَّنِي بَرَاءٌ مِمَّا تَعْبُدُونَ ۝ إِلَّا الَّذِي فَطَرَنِي فَإِنَّهُ سَيَهْدِينِ ۝ وَجَعَلَهَا كَلِمَةً بَاقِيَةً فِي عَقِبِهِ لَعَلَّهُمْ يَرْجِعُونَ ۝﴾، وقوله تعالى: ﴿قُلْ يَا أَهْلَ الْكِتَابِ تَعَالَوْا إِلَىٰ كَلِمَةٍ سَوَاءٍ بَيْنَنَا وَبَيْنَكُمْ أَلَّا نَعْبُدَ إِلَّا اللَّهَ وَلَا نُشْرِكَ بِهِ شَيْئًا وَلَا يَتَّخِذَ بَعْضُنَا بَعْضًا أَرْبَابًا مِنْ دُونِ اللَّهِ فَإِنْ تَوَلَّوْا فَقُولُوا اشْهَدُوا بِأَنَّا مُسْلِمُونَ﴾.

والرب هو المعبود، والدليل قوله تعالى: ﴿يَٰٓأَيُّهَا ٱلنَّاسُ ٱعْبُدُوا۟ رَبَّكُمُ ٱلَّذِى خَلَقَكُمْ وَٱلَّذِينَ مِن قَبْلِكُمْ لَعَلَّكُمْ تَتَّقُونَ ۝ ٱلَّذِى جَعَلَ لَكُمُ ٱلْأَرْضَ فِرَٰشًا وَٱلسَّمَآءَ بِنَآءً وَأَنزَلَ مِنَ ٱلسَّمَآءِ مَآءً فَأَخْرَجَ بِهِۦ مِنَ ٱلثَّمَرَٰتِ رِزْقًا لَّكُمْ فَلَا تَجْعَلُوا۟ لِلَّهِ أَندَادًا وَأَنتُمْ تَعْلَمُونَ ۝﴾. قال ابن كثير: الخالق لهذه الأشياء هو المستحق للعبادة.

وأنواع العبادة التي أمر الله بها مثل الإسلام، والإيمان، والإحسان، ومنه الدعاء، والخوف، والرجاء، والتوكل، والرغبة، والرهبة، والخشوع، والخشية، والإنابة، والاستعانة، والاستعاذة، والاستغاثة، والذبح، والنذر، وغير ذلك من العبادة التي أمر الله بها، كلها لله، والدليل قوله تعالى: ﴿وَأَنَّ ٱلْمَسَٰجِدَ لِلَّهِ فَلَا تَدْعُوا۟ مَعَ ٱللَّهِ أَحَدًا﴾.

فمن صرف منها شيئا لغير الله فهو مشرك كافر، والدليل قوله تعالى: ﴿وَمَن يَدْعُ مَعَ ٱللَّهِ إِلَٰهًا ءَاخَرَ لَا بُرْهَٰنَ لَهُۥ بِهِۦ فَإِنَّمَا حِسَابُهُۥ عِندَ رَبِّهِۦٓ إِنَّهُۥ لَا يُفْلِحُ ٱلْكَٰفِرُونَ﴾. وفي الحديث: الدعاء مخ العبادة. والدليل قوله تعالى: ﴿وَقَالَ رَبُّكُمُ ٱدْعُونِىٓ أَسْتَجِبْ لَكُمْ إِنَّ ٱلَّذِينَ يَسْتَكْبِرُونَ عَنْ عِبَادَتِى سَيَدْخُلُونَ جَهَنَّمَ دَاخِرِينَ﴾.

ودليل الخوف قوله تعالى: ﴿فَلَا تَخَافُوهُمْ وَخَافُونِ إِن كُنتُم مُّؤْمِنِينَ﴾.

ودليل الرجاء قوله تعالى: ﴿فَمَن كَانَ يَرْجُوا۟ لِقَآءَ رَبِّهِۦ فَلْيَعْمَلْ عَمَلًا صَٰلِحًا وَلَا يُشْرِكْ بِعِبَادَةِ رَبِّهِۦٓ أَحَدًا﴾.

ودليل التوكل قوله تعالى: ﴿وَعَلَى ٱللَّهِ فَتَوَكَّلُوٓا۟ إِن كُنتُم مُّؤْمِنِينَ﴾؛ ﴿وَمَن يَتَوَكَّلْ عَلَى ٱللَّهِ فَهُوَ حَسْبُهُۥٓ﴾.

ودليل الرغبة والرهبة والخشوع قوله تعالى: ﴿إِنَّهُمْ كَانُوا۟ يُسَٰرِعُونَ فِى ٱلْخَيْرَٰتِ وَيَدْعُونَنَا رَغَبًا وَرَهَبًا وَكَانُوا۟ لَنَا خَٰشِعِينَ﴾.

ودليل الخشية قوله تعالى: ﴿فَلَا تَخْشَوْهُمْ وَٱخْشَوْنِ﴾، الآية.

ودليل الإنابة قوله تعالى: ﴿وَأَنِيبُوٓا۟ إِلَىٰ رَبِّكُمْ وَأَسْلِمُوا۟ لَهُۥ مِن قَبْلِ أَن يَأْتِيَكُمُ ٱلْعَذَابُ ثُمَّ لَا تُنصَرُونَ﴾، الآية.

الثالثة: أن من أطاع الرسول ووحد الله لا يجوز له موالاة من حاد الله ورسوله ولو كان أقرب قريب، والدليل قوله تعالى: ﴿لَّا تَجِدُ قَوْمًا يُؤْمِنُونَ بِاللَّهِ وَالْيَوْمِ الْآخِرِ يُوَادُّونَ مَنْ حَادَّ اللَّهَ وَرَسُولَهُ وَلَوْ كَانُوا آبَاءَهُمْ أَوْ أَبْنَاءَهُمْ أَوْ إِخْوَانَهُمْ أَوْ عَشِيرَتَهُمْ أُولَٰئِكَ كَتَبَ فِي قُلُوبِهِمُ الْإِيمَانَ وَأَيَّدَهُم بِرُوحٍ مِّنْهُ وَيُدْخِلُهُمْ جَنَّاتٍ تَجْرِي مِن تَحْتِهَا الْأَنْهَارُ خَالِدِينَ فِيهَا رَضِيَ اللَّهُ عَنْهُمْ وَرَضُوا عَنْهُ أُولَٰئِكَ حِزْبُ اللَّهِ أَلَا إِنَّ حِزْبَ اللَّهِ هُمُ الْمُفْلِحُونَ ﴾.

اعلم أرشدك الله لطاعته: أن الحنيفية ملة إبراهيم أن تعبد الله وحده مخلصا له الدين، وبذلك أمر الله جميع الناس وخلقهم لها، قال تعالى: ﴿وَمَا خَلَقْتُ الْجِنَّ وَالْإِنسَ إِلَّا لِيَعْبُدُونِ ﴾، ومعنى يعبدون: يوحدون.

وأعظم ما أمر الله به: التوحيد، وهو إفراد الله بالعبادة. وأعظم ما نهى عنه: الشرك، وهو دعوة غيره معه، والدليل قوله تعالى: ﴿وَاعْبُدُوا اللَّهَ وَلَا تُشْرِكُوا بِهِ شَيْئًا ﴾.

فإذا قيل لك: ما الأصول الثلاثة التي يجب على الإنسان معرفتها؟ فقل: معرفة العبد ربه، ودينه، ونبيه محمدا صلى الله عليه وسلم.

فإذا قيل لك: من ربك؟ فقل: ربي الله رباني وربى جميع العالمين بنعمته، وهو معبودي، ليس لي معبود سواه. والدليل قوله تعالى: ﴿الْحَمْدُ لِلَّهِ رَبِّ الْعَالَمِينَ ﴾، وكل ما سوى الله عالم، وأنا واحد من ذلك العالم.

فإذا قيل لك: بم عرفت ربك؟ فقل: بآياته ومخلوقاته. ومن آياته: الليل، والنهار، والشمس، والقمر. ومن مخلوقاته: السماوات السبع، والأرضون السبع، ومن فيهن، وما بينهما. والدليل قوله تعالى: ﴿وَمِنْ آيَاتِهِ اللَّيْلُ وَالنَّهَارُ وَالشَّمْسُ وَالْقَمَرُ لَا تَسْجُدُوا لِلشَّمْسِ وَلَا لِلْقَمَرِ وَاسْجُدُوا لِلَّهِ الَّذِي خَلَقَهُنَّ إِن كُنتُمْ إِيَّاهُ تَعْبُدُونَ ﴾، وقوله تعالى: ﴿إِنَّ رَبَّكُمُ اللَّهُ الَّذِي خَلَقَ السَّمَاوَاتِ وَالْأَرْضَ فِي سِتَّةِ أَيَّامٍ ثُمَّ اسْتَوَىٰ عَلَى الْعَرْشِ يُغْشِي اللَّيْلَ النَّهَارَ يَطْلُبُهُ حَثِيثًا وَالشَّمْسَ وَالْقَمَرَ وَالنُّجُومَ مُسَخَّرَاتٍ بِأَمْرِهِ أَلَا لَهُ الْخَلْقُ وَالْأَمْرُ تَبَارَكَ اللَّهُ رَبُّ الْعَالَمِينَ ﴾.

APPENDIX III
THE COMPLETE ARABIC TEXT (UNVOWELED)

بسم الله الرحمن الرحيم

اعلم رحمك الله أنه يجب علينا تعلم أربع مسائل: الأولى: العلم، وهو معرفة الله، ومعرفة نبيه، ومعرفة دين الإسلام بالأدلة. الثانية: العمل به. الثالثة: الدعوة إليه. الرابعة: الصبر على الأذى فيه.

والدليل قوله تعالى: بسم الله الرحمن الرحيم، ﴿وَٱلْعَصْرِ ١ إِنَّ ٱلْإِنسَٰنَ لَفِى خُسْرٍ ٢ إِلَّا ٱلَّذِينَ ءَامَنُوا۟ وَعَمِلُوا۟ ٱلصَّٰلِحَٰتِ وَتَوَاصَوْا۟ بِٱلْحَقِّ وَتَوَاصَوْا۟ بِٱلصَّبْرِ ٣﴾. قال الشافعي رحمه الله تعالى: لو ما أنزل الله حجة على خلقه إلا هذه السورة لكفتهم.

وقال البخاري رحمه الله تعالى: باب العلم قبل القول والعمل، والدليل قوله تعالى: ﴿فَٱعْلَمْ أَنَّهُۥ لَآ إِلَٰهَ إِلَّا ٱللَّهُ وَٱسْتَغْفِرْ لِذَنۢبِكَ﴾، فبدأ بالعلم قبل القول والعمل.

اعلم رحمك الله أنه يجب على كل مسلم ومسلمة تعلم ثلاث هذه المسائل والعمل بهن:

الأولى: أن الله خلقنا ورزقنا ولم يتركنا هملا، بل أرسل إلينا رسولا، فمن أطاعه دخل الجنة، ومن عصاه دخل النار، والدليل قوله تعالى: ﴿إِنَّآ أَرْسَلْنَآ إِلَيْكُمْ رَسُولًا شَٰهِدًا عَلَيْكُمْ كَمَآ أَرْسَلْنَآ إِلَىٰ فِرْعَوْنَ رَسُولًا ١٥ فَعَصَىٰ فِرْعَوْنُ ٱلرَّسُولَ فَأَخَذْنَٰهُ أَخْذًا وَبِيلًا ١٦﴾.

الثانية: أن الله لا يرضى أن يشرك معه في عبادته أحد، لا ملك مقرب، ولا نبي مرسل، والدليل قوله تعالى: ﴿وَأَنَّ ٱلْمَسَٰجِدَ لِلَّهِ فَلَا تَدْعُوا۟ مَعَ ٱللَّهِ أَحَدًا﴾.

من أسانيد رسالة «ثلاثة الأصول وأدلتها»

قال الخطَّاء الفقير إلى رحمة ربه أبو العباس موسى الطويل الأمريكي ثم المكي ــ عفا الله عنه ــ : أروي رسالة ثلاثة الأصول وأدلتها وغيرها من كتب الإمام المجدد محمد بن عبدالوهاب التميمي ــ رحمه الله ــ عن عدد من المشايخ السلفيين الأثبات إجازة.

منهم شيخي العلامة يحيى بن عثمان المدرّس ــ حفظه الله ــ ؛

وهو يرويها عن الشيخ العلامة أحمد بن يحيى النجمي ــ حفظه الله ــ مدبَّجًا؛

كلاهما عن الشيخ العلامة عبدالرحمن بن عبدالحي بن عبدالكبير الكتّاني ولد صاحب فهرس الفهارس؛

عن الشيخ العلامة أبي بكر ابن محمد عارف بن عبدالقادر خوقير المكي (ت١٣٤٩)؛

عن الشيخ العلامة أحمد بن إبراهيم بن عيسى النجدي (ت١٣٢٩)؛

عن الشيخ العلامة عبدالرحمن بن حسن الحفيد (ت١٢٨٥)؛

عن جده الإمام ــ رحمهم الله جميعًا.

وبذلك ــ بفضل الله تعالى ــ قد اتصل إسنادي وإسنادُ مَن سمع مني شيئًا من هذه الكتب النافعة والرسائل المفيدة، ولله الحمد، وصلى الله وسلم وبارك على نبينا محمد وعلى آله وصحبه أجمعين.

بأسنى ووحدكذب بالبعث كفر والدليل قوله تعالى زعم الذين كفروا ان لن يبعثوا قل بلى وربي لتبعثن وارسل الله جميع الرسل مبشرين ومنذ والدليل قوله تعالى رسلا مبشرين ومنذرين لئلا يكون للناس حجة بعد الرسل الآية واولهم نوح عليه السلام واخرهم محمد صلى الله عليه وسلم وهو خاتم النبيين لا نبي بعده والدليل قوله تعالى ما كان محمد ابا احد من رجالكم الآية والدليل على ان اولهم نوح قوله تعالى انا اوحينا اليك كما اوحينا الى نوح والنبيين من بعده وكل امة بعث الله اليها رسولا من نوح الى محمد يأمرهم بعبادة الله وحده وينهاهم عن عبادة الطاغوت والدليل قوله تعالى ولقد بعثنا في كل امة رسولا ان عبدوا الله واجتنبوا الطاغوت وافترض من الله على جميع العباد ان يكفروا بالطاغوت و يؤمنوا بالله تعالى قال ابن القيم رحمه الله تعالى معنى الطاغوت ما جاوز به العبد حده من معبود او متبوع او مطاع والطواغيت كثيرة ورؤسهم خمسة ابليس لعنه الله ومن عبد وهو راض ومن دعا الناس الى عبادة نفسه ومن حكم بغير ما انزل الله ومن ادعى شيئا من الغيب والدليل قوله تعالى لا اكراه في الدين قد تبين الرشد من الغي فمن يكفر بالطاغوت ويؤمن بالله الآية وهذا معنى لا اله الا الله وفي الحديث راس الامر الاسلام وعموده الصلاة وذروة سنامه الجهاد في سبيل الله عز وجل والله اعلم تمت ثلاثة الاصول وصلى الله على محمد والحمد لله رب العالمين وسلم تسليما كثيرا

بلد الشرك الى بلد الاسلام وفي باقية الى ان تقوم الساعة والدليل قوله تعالى ان الذين توفاهم الملائكة ظالمي انفسهم قالوا فيم كنتم الى قوله وكان الله عفوا غفورا وقوله يا عبادي الذين امنوا ان ارضي واسعة الاية قال البغوي رحمه الله تعالى سبب نزول هذه الاية في المسلمين الذين بمكة لم يهاجروا ونادهم الله باسم الايمان والدليل على الهجرة من السنة قوله صلى الله عليه وسلم لا تنقطع الهجرة حتى تنقطع التوبه ولا تنقطع التوبه حتى تطلع الشمس من مغربها فان استقر بالمدينة هو وبقية شرايع الاسلام مثل الزكاة والصوم والحج والجهاد والاذان والامر بالمعروف والنهي عن المنكر واقفه على هذا من اعشر سنين وتوفي صلى الله عليه وسلم ودينه باق وهذا دينه الذي لا خير الا دل الامة عليه ولا شر الا حذرها عنه والخير الذي دل عليه التوحيد وما يحبه الله ويرضاه والشر الذي حذر عنه الشرك بالله وجميع ما يكرهه الله ويأباه بعثه الله الى الناس كافة وافترض الله طاعته على جميع الثقلين الجن والانس والدليل قوله تعالى قل يا ايها الناس اني رسول الله اليكم جميعا واكمل الله له الدين والدليل قوله تعالى اليوم اكملت لكم دينكم واتممت عليكم نعمتي الاية والدليل على موته قوله تعالى انك ميت وانهم ميتون الاية والناس اذا ماتوا يبعثون والدليل قوله تعالى منها خلقناكم وفيها نعيدكم ومنها نخرجكم تارة اخرى وقوله تعالى والله انبتكم من الارض نباتا الاية وبعد البعث محاسبون ومجزيون باعمالهم والدليل قوله تعالى ليجزي الذين اساؤوا بما عملوا ويجزي الذين احسنوا بالحسنى

قال فأخبرني عن الإحسان قال أن تعبد الله كأنك تراه فإن لم تكن تراه فإنه يراك قال صدقت قال أخبرني عن الساعة قال ما المسؤول عنها بأعلم من السائل قال أخبرني عن إمارتها قال أن تلد الأمة ربتها وأن ترى الحفاة العراة العالة رعاء الشاء يتطاولون في البنيان فمضى فلبثنا مليا فقال صلى الله عليه وسلم يا عمر أتدرون من السائل قلنا الله ورسوله أعلم قال هذا جبريل أتاكم يعلمكم من دينكم الأصل الثالث معرفة نبيكم محمد صلى الله عليه وسلم وهو محمد بن عبد الله بن عبد المطلب بن هاشم وهاشم من قريش وقريش من العرب والعرب من ذرية اسماعيل بن ابراهيم الخليل عليه وعلى نبينا أفضل الصلاة والسلام ولد له العمر ثلاث وستون سنه منها أربعون قبل النبوة وثلاث وعشرون نبيا رسولا نبي بأقرأ وأرسل بالمدثر وبلده مكة بعثه الله بالنذارة عن الشرك ويدعو الى التوحيد والدليل قوله تعالى يا أيها المدثر قم فانذر الى قوله تعالى ولربك فاصبر ومعنى قم فانذر يعني ينذر عن الشرك ويدعو الى التوحيد وربك فكبر أي عظمه بالتوحيد وثيابك فطهر أي طهر أعمالك عن الشرك والرجز فاهجر الرجز الأصنام وهجرانها تركها والبراءة منها وأهلها ومعاداتها وأهلها وفراقها وأهلها أخذ على هذا عشر سنين يدعو الى التوحيد وبعد العشر عرج به الى السماء وفرضت عليه الصلوات الخمس وصلى في مكة ثلاث سنين وبعدها أمر بالهجرة الى المدينة والهجرة في الانتقال

عن الطريق والحياء شعبة من الإيمان فالمجموع كله ستة أن توقن بالله وملائكته وكتبه ورسله واليوم الآخر والقدر خيره وشره كله من الله والدليل على هذه الأركان الستة قوله تعالى ليس البر أن تولوا وجوهكم قبل المشرق والمغرب ولكن البر من آمن بالله واليوم الآخر الآية ودليل القدر قوله تعالى إنا كل شيء خلقناه بقدر المرتبة الثالثة الإحسان ركن واحد والدليل قوله تعالى ومن يسلم وجهه لله وهو محسن الآية وهو أن تعبد الله وحده كأنك تراه فإن لم تكن تراه فإنه يراك وقوله تعالى أن الله مع الذين اتقوا والذين هم محسنون وقوله تعالى ومن يتوكل على الله فهو حسبه وقوله تعالى وتوكل على العزيز الرحيم الذي يراك حين تقوم وقوله تعالى وما تكون في شأن وما تتلو منه من قرآن ولا تعملون من عمل إلا كنا عليكم شهودا الآية والدليل من السنة حديث جبريل المشهور عن عمر رضي الله عنه قال بينما نحن جلوس عند النبي صلى الله عليه وسلم إذ طلع علينا رجل شديد بياض الثياب شديد سواد الشعر لا يرى عليه أثر السفر ولا يعرفه منا أحد فجلس إلى النبي صلى الله عليه وسلم فأسند ركبتيه إلى ركبتيه ووضع كفيه على فخذيه فقال يا محمد أخبرني عن الإسلام قال أن تشهد أن لا إله إلا الله وأن محمد رسول الله وتقيم الصلاة وتؤتي الزكاة وتصوم رمضان وتحج البيت إن استطعت إليه سبيلا قال صدقت فعجبنا له يسأله ويصدقه قال فأخبرني عن الإيمان قال أن تؤمن بالله وملائكته وكتبه ورسله واليوم الآخر والقدر قال صدقت

قال

والخلوص من الشرك وهو ثلاث مراتب الاسلام والايمان والاحسان وكل
مرتبة لها اركان فاركان الاسلام خمسة والدليل من العشرة حديث
ابن عمر رضي الله عنهما قال قال رسول الله صلى الله عليه وسلم
بني الاسلام على خمس شهادة ان لا اله الا الله وان محمدا رسول الله
واقام الصلاة وايتاء الزكاة وصوم رمضان وحج بيت الله الحرام
فدليل الشهادة قوله تعالى شهد الله انه لا اله الا هو والملايكة واو
لوا العلم الايه ومعناها لا معبود بحق الا الله وحده النفي لا اله نافيا
بجميع ما يعبد من دون الله الا الله مثبتا العبادة لله وحده لا شريك
له كلا في عبادته كما انه ليس له شريك في ملكه وتفسيرها
الذي يوضحها قوله تعالى واذ قال ابراهيم لابيه وقومه
انني براء مما تعبدون الا الذي فطرني الايه وقوله تعالى قل يا اهل
الكتاب تعالوا الى كلمة سواء بيننا وبينكم ودليل
محمد رسول الله قوله تعالى لقد جاءكم رسول من انفسكم الايه ومعنى
شهادة ان محمد رسول الله طاعته فيما امر وتصديقه فيما اخبر
واجتناب ما عنه نهى وزجر وان لا يعبد الله الا بما شرع ودليل الصلاة
والزكاة وتفسير التوحيد قوله تعالى وما امروا الا ليعبد الله مخلصين له الدين
حنفاء ويقيموا الصلاة ويؤتوا الزكاة وذلك دين القيم ودليل
الصوم قوله تعالى يا ايها الذين امنوا كتب عليكم الصيام كما كتب على
الذين من قبلكم الايه ودليل الحج قوله تعالى ولله على الناس حج البيت
من استطاع اليه سبيلا المرتبة الثانية الايمان وهو بضع
وسبعون شعبة اعلاها قول لا اله الا الله وادنا ها اماطة الاذى

والاستعانة والاستعاذة والاستغاثة والذبح والنذر والتوبة وغير ذلك من أنواع العبادة التي أمر الله بها كلها لله تعالى والدليل قوله تعالى وأن المساجد لله فلا تدعوا مع الله أحداً فمن صرف منها شيئاً لغير الله تعالى فهو مشرك كافر والدليل قوله تعالى ومن يدع مع الله إلهاً آخر لا برهان له به فإنما حسابه عند ربه إنه لا يفلح الكافرون وفي الحديث الدعاء مخ العبادة والدليل قوله تعالى وقال ربكم ادعوني أستجب لكم الآية ودليل الخوف قوله تعالى فلا تخافوهم وخافوني إن كنتم مؤمنين ودليل الرجاء قوله تعالى فمن كان يرجو لقاء ربه فليعمل عملاً صالحاً الآية ودليل التوكل قوله تعالى وعلى الله فتوكلوا إن كنتم مؤمنين وقوله تعالى ومن يتوكل على الله فهو حسبه ودليل الرغبة والرهبة والخشوع قوله تعالى إنهم كانوا يسارعون في الخيرات ويدعوننا رغباً ورهباً وكانوا لنا خاشعين ودليل الخشية قوله تعالى فلا تخشوهم واخشون إن كنتم مؤمنين ودليل الإنابة قوله تعالى وأنيبوا إلى ربكم وأسلموا له الآية ودليل الاستعانة قوله تعالى إياك نعبد وإياك نستعين ودليل الاستعاذة قوله تعالى قل أعوذ برب الناس ملك الناس إله الناس ودليل الاستغاثة قوله تعالى إذ تستغيثون ربكم فاستجاب لكم الآية ودليل الذبح قوله تعالى قل إن صلاتي ونسكي ومحياي ومماتي لله رب العالمين لا شريك له الآية وفي السنة لعن الله من ذبح لغير الله ودليل النذر قوله تعالى يوفون بالنذر الآية ودليل التوبة قوله وتوبوا إلى الله جميعاً الآية الأصل الثاني معرفة دين الإسلام بالأدلة وهو الاستسلام لله بالتوحيد والانقياد له بالطاعة والخلوص

١٣٤

بوادون من جاد الله ورسوله الايه اعلم ان شرك الله لحاجته ان الحنيفية ملة ابراهيم ان تعبد الله وحده تخلص له الدين كما قال وما خلقت الجن والانس الا ليعبدون اي الايه ومعنى يعبدون يوحدون واعظم ما امر الله به التوحيد وهو افراد الله تعالى بالعبادة واعظم ما نهى عنه الشرك وهو دعوة غيره معه والدليل قوله تعالى واعبدوا الله ولا تشركوا به شيا فاذا قيل لك ما الاصول الثلاثة التي يجب على الانسان معرفتها فقل معرفة العبد ربه ودينه ونبيه محمد صلى الله عليه وسلم فاذا قيل لك من ربك فقل ربي الله الذي رباني وربى جميع العالمين بنعمته وهو معبودي ليس لي معبود سواه والدليل قوله تعالى الحمد لله رب العالمين وكل ما سواه عالم وانا واحد من ذلك العالم واذا قيل لك بما عرفت ربك فقل بآياته وخلقه ومن آياته الليل والنهار والشمس والقمر ومن مخلوقاته السموات السبع وما فيهن والارضين السبع ومن فيهن وما بينهما والدليل قوله تعالى ومن آياته الليل والنهار والشمس والقمر لا تسجدوا والدليل قوله تعالى ان ربكم الله الذي خلق السموات والارض في ستة ايام ثم استوى على العرش الايه والرب هو المعبود والدليل قوله تعالى يا ايها الناس اعبدوا ربكم الذي خلقكم والذين من قبلكم بآيتي قال ابن كثير رحمه الله تعالى الخالق لهذه الاشياء هو المستحق للعبادة فانواع العبادة التي امر الله بها مثل الاسلام والايمان والاحسان ومنه الدعاء والخوف والرجاء والتوكل والرغبة والرهبة والخشوع والخشية والانابة

ليس

بسم الله الرحمن الرحيم وبه نستعين

اعلم رحمك الله انه يجب علينا تعلم اربع مسائل الأولى العلم وهو معرفة الله ومعرفة نبيه ومعرفة دين الاسلام بالأدلة الثانية العمل به العمل به الثالثة الدعوة اليه الرابعة الصبر على الأذى فيه والدليل قوله تعالى بسم الله الرحمن الرحيم والعصر ان الانسان لفي خسر الا الذين آمنوا وعملوا الصالحات وتواصوا بالحق وتواصوا بالصبر قال الشافعي رحمه الله تعالى لو ما انزل الله حجة على خلقه الا هذه السورة لكفتهم قال البخاري رحمه الله تعالى باب العلم قبل القول والعمل والدليل قوله تعالى فاعلم انه لا اله الا الله فبدا بالعلم قبل القول والعمل

اعلم رحمك الله ان الله وجب على كل مسلم ومسلمة تعلم ثلاث هذه المسائل والعمل بهن اولها ان الله خلقنا ورزقنا ولم يتركنا هملا وارسل الينا رسولا فمن اطاعه دخل الجنة ومن عصاه دخل النار والدليل قوله تعالى انا ارسلنا اليكم رسولا شاهدا عليكم كما ارسلنا الى فرعون رسولا الثانية ان الله لا يرضى ان يشرك معه في عبادته احد لا نبي مرسل ولا ملك مقرب والدليل قوله تعالى وان المساجد لله فلا تدعوا مع الله احدا الثالثة ان من اطاع الرسول ووحد الله لا يجوز له موالاة من حاد الله ورسوله ولو كان اقرب قريب والدليل قوله تعالى لا تجد قوما يؤمنون بالله واليوم الآخر

يوادون

... ثلاثة الأصول والقواعد الأربع وشروط الصلاة وأركانها

وواجباتها وسنتها وما يتعلق بذلك من

الأدلة تأليف الشيخ الإمام محمد

بن عبد الوهاب اجزل ...

الله الأجر و ...

الثواب و ...

أحسن المآب ...

وأدخله جنة بغير ...

حساب ...

أ ...

قائدة

الشيخ عبد الرحمن بن حسن رحمه الله وعفى عنه في ... كلام له على ...

... لا إله إلا الله في التهذيب قال قلت لا بد في شهادة أن لا

... الأكمه من سبعة شروط لا تنفع قائلها إلا بها أحدهما العلم المنافي

... الثاني اليقين المنافي للشك والثالث القبول المنافي للرد الرابع

... الانقياد المنافي للترك الخامس الإخلاص المنافي للشرك السادس الصدق

... المنافي للكذب السابع المحبة المنافي له ... صلوات الله على محمد ...

خزانة : طارق الهويطب

البلد : الرياض

52372462R00083

Made in the USA
Middletown, DE
11 July 2019